Speed Reading

The Oxford Centre for the Mind:

Quick Courses

Gary Lorrison

Speed Reading

The Oxford Centre for the Mind

Quick Courses

Effective strategies to read at much higher speeds than you do now and get on top of all of your reading

Gary Lorrison

Oxford Mind Publishing

THE OXFORD CENTRE FOR THE MIND LIMITED

#123,
94, London Road
Headington
Oxford OX3 9FN

email: info@oxfordmind.co.uk
web: www.oxfordmind.co.uk

Oxford Mind Publishing is a division of the Oxford Centre for the Mind Limited.

ISBN-13: 978-1500117214

ISBN-10: 1500117218

About the Author

Having studied law at Cambridge, Gary Lorrison started off his career working in London as a solicitor but quickly saw the light and left the legal profession to develop his interest in the mind. He quickly earned two degrees in philosophy but found himself focusing on how one could use the techniques of philosophy, psychology and science to run one's mind more effectively.

Since 2003, he has been actively involved in running personal development training programmes to help people improve their mental performance. He has a special interest in memory training and other ways of helping people absorb information as well as the techniques of logical, critical and analytical thinking and the limits of human rationality.

In his spare time he enjoys walking in the countryside, takes a keen interest in music playing a number of instruments and is an occasional skydiver.

He lives on a farm near Oxford with four dogs, three cats, three ducks, six geese, about five hundred sheep and the odd human being.

Testimonials

Testimonials for our seminars: -

"Excellent - best course I have been on in ages - thought provoking and insightful"

"Great workshop. Coach created a very relaxing, easy and open atmosphere. Coach was helpful and had a very pleasant way of interacting with us"

"I am very happy I came to this workshop. It was good value for money and provided very useful skills that I know will help my studies"

"It's a great course - I would recommend you go on it"

"Good fun and value for money"

"Do it! - Very interesting and a good approach to de-stressing about work levels etc."

"It really works, especially the visualisation techniques"

For information on all of the courses run by the Oxford Centre for the Mind please visit our website:

www.oxfordmind.co.uk

Contents

ONE

INTRODUCTION

Aims

The aim of the Speed Reading Quick Course is to take you from wherever you are now in your reading abilities and to turn you into a world class reader by showing you how to read at speeds significantly faster than you do now.

You will also learn to concentrate more on what you are reading, so that you will take in and understand more. You will learn how to manage any reading tasks or assignments so that you can get the most out of them in the smallest amount of time. And because of all this you will, we hope, find reading a much more enjoyable activity than you do now.

Benefits of speed reading

The benefits of being able to read much more quickly should be self-evident. By learning to read more quickly, you will be able to absorb more new information in less time, expand your knowledge base and enhance your abilities in a wide variety of situations.

As with other areas of cognitive training such as developing your memory, the ability to read at speed will give you a competitive edge at work, raising your efficiency as well as your earning potential.

If you have a certain amount of material that you have to read regularly, you will also free up time to devote to other things and, of course, you will be able to read more. These factors may awaken an interest in new areas, leading to a much richer and fuller life. Your expanded knowledge base could also lead to an increase in your general level of intelligence.

We suggest that you spend some time contemplating what the specific benefits to you of developing the ability to read at high speeds will be and note them down. Identifying these factors will help you to stay motivated.

Reading potential

The following table sets out a ranking of different reading speeds in words per minute (wpm): -

Poor	10 - 100
Below average	100 - 200
Average	200 - 400
Above average	400 - 600
Good	600 - 800
Top 1%	800 – 1000
Top 0.1%	1000 +

The United Nations defines functional literacy as being able to read at 400 wpm.

By the end of the course, you should easily fall into the top 1% of readers. In a course on skim reading that was taught at North West University in the USA, the majority of the people who took the course were able to read at speeds of 2,000 wpm when they had finished.

One per cent were able to read at 20,000 wpm and one girl was able to read at speeds of up to 80,000 wpm. Do note, however, that skim reading is not the same as speed reading. It is possible to skim read faster than speed read, because your aims are different. The difference between the two will become apparent during this course.

Under competition conditions, speed readers are required to read a passage and are then tested on their understanding by a panel of experts. Speeds of up to 3,850 wpm have been recorded.

If you could read at this speed you would be able to read ten pages of an average book every minute, one hundred pages in ten minutes, and six hundred pages in an hour!

You would be able to read most books from start to finish in under an hour, and there would be very few that you wouldn't be able to finish in two hours. Compare that to how long it takes you at the moment, and consider how much more knowledge and information you would be able to take in as a result of such an increase in reading ability.

By following the Speed Reading Quick Course you will certainly be able to read faster. To achieve the highest reading speeds will require practice and dedication. Think of speed reading like running. With just a little practice you can run faster and not much effort is required to maintain that standard.

However, to be an Olympic standard runner you would have to put in a lot of practice and once you had reached that level, you would have to carry on working to maintain it. Reading at 1,000 wpm is like being a good standard runner. Reading at 3,000-4,000 wpm is the reading equivalent of being an Olympic runner.

If you want to be one of the fastest readers in the world, it will require practice to get there and work to maintain that level.

In case you have your doubts about your ability to read at higher speeds take a piece of card and cover up the sentence at the top of the following page. Reveal it and then cover it up again as quickly as you can – revealing it for about one third of a second. If you can read all of it, then you should certainly be able to increase your reading speed to about 1,000 wpm. Even if you couldn't read all of it, as long as you could see it all, you should also be able to achieve good results.

List specific benefits
Stay motivated.

Can you read this phrase?

Course structure

This course is structured as follows: -

In part one, we will give you advice on how to become a better reader by altering your current reading practices, adopting good habits and eliminating bad ones.

In part two, we shall show you specifically how to read at speeds of up to 1,000 wpm, by explaining how the eye works, giving you strategies for controlling your eye movement, and taking in more words at a time. There are also a number of exercises to help you consistently reach these speeds.

Reading at speeds faster than 1,000 wpm requires some new techniques and in part three we will outline these and again show you how to practise them.

Finally in part four, we will discuss intelligent reading techniques that you can apply to specific types of reading, so that whatever it is you want to read, from a book to a newspaper article to a business report, you will be able to get the most out of it in the least time.

Practical nature of the course

Remember as you go through this course that it is designed to be practical, not theoretical. You should do all of the exercises when we indicate. If you don't, you might gain an intellectual understanding of what to do, but you will not gain the benefits you will from actually doing the exercises. Learning to speed read does require practice.

Onword

The following section, 'Becoming a better reader', will provide a solid foundation for the rest of the course, by outlining various strategies you can use to identify and eliminate any bad reading habits you may currently have and advice on various aspects of good reading practice.

PART 1

READING FUNDAMENTALS

TWO

BECOMING A BETTER READER

Aim

The aim of this section is to make you a better reader generally by changing certain beliefs about the way you should read, making you aware of certain problems and bad habits you might have and helping you to eliminate them. We will also tell you about what you can do to ensure that you are always in the best reading state, and help you establish better habits.

Problems and bad habits

There are a number of reading habits that people fall into that slow them down, reducing their ability to concentrate on what they are reading, and hampering their enjoyment. With a little commitment and practice these habits can be eliminated. Other problems can be eradicated by changing one's mental approach to the material being read.

Subvocalisation

Subvocalisation can be one of two things: either mouthing words to yourself as you read, or hearing them in your head.

Dealing with the first element, mouthing to yourself: this will be a problem if you want to read very quickly because generally not even the fastest speakers can speak at more than 300 wpm. Therefore, by mouthing what you are reading to yourself, you will inevitably be limiting the speed at which you can read. The solution to this, in the initial stages, is consciously to refrain from doing so, and speed up your reading till you reach a speed that is impossible to mouth.

Plan to read for twenty minutes every day for the next three weeks. During this period make sure that you refrain from mouthing while you are reading. If you can manage this for three weeks, you should be well on your way to eliminating this habit.

It is possible that you may not be aware that you mouth when you read, as you may do it subconsciously. If you are not sure whether you mouth words, ask someone to watch you as you read. They will be able to tell you.

The second type of subvocalisation is when you hear words in your head as you read. This is less of a problem than mouthing as it is possible to hear at a faster rate than you can speak, and so you should be able to hear every word inside your head and still read at speed. You should try to reduce your reliance on hearing the words in your head as much as you can, though. Try instead to take in meaning from the visual appearance of the words and push what you hear back into your subconscious as much as possible. You can do this by being completely relaxed and focused, something we discuss below.

Finger Pointing

Finger pointing is moving your finger over the page as you read it, using it as a visual guide. This is usually perceived as a problem because of the way reading is taught in school. You start off by reading one word at a time, pointing to each word as you do so. As you get more fluent, you are encouraged to stop using your finger because it is supposed to slow you down. The better readers are usually the first to stop using their fingers while the slower ones are the ones who take longer to give up the habit.

However, the reality is that using some form of visual guide, such as your finger, makes it much easier for you to point your eye exactly where you want.

Try this exercise. Get a partner to sit facing you and then ask them to move their eyes slowly around in a large circle. Watch their eyes very closely. The movements will be very jerky and not particularly circular. Now ask them to do the same but to hold an arm out in front of them and then move it around in a big circle, pointing their index finger up and using it as a guide for their eyes to focus on. Again watch their eyes closely. This time their eye movements will be much smoother and more circular.

This exercise demonstrates that you can control your eyes much better if you use your finger as a pointer to focus on. There is no reason why this should slow you down, because all you need to do to speed up your reading if you are using your finger as a pointer, is to move your finger faster. We will discuss this in more detail in the following sections.

Regression

Regression is when you consciously return to material you have previously read. Clearly, any time you spend re-reading material is time that you are not reading new material, so doing this will slow you down. If you do regress, you need to ask yourself why you are re-reading the material and whether it is compatible with your goals.

If you are reading for pleasure and you come across a particularly pleasing passage, you may want to read it again. There is nothing wrong with doing so. You should just be aware that it will slow you down.

However, there may be other reasons why you re-read the same passage. You might be re-reading material with which you are familiar and comfortable in order to avoid moving on to new material that you think will be more difficult.

Alternatively, you may be re-reading something because you find it particularly difficult to understand. It is generally better to read a passage in one go without re-reading any of it, because you will be able to derive more from the surrounding context than you will by reading one section over and over in isolation from the rest of the text. We will deal with this further in the Intelligent Reading section.

Now that you know about regression, try to become aware of it whenever you do it. You can then make a conscious decision as to whether you want to read a particular piece again or not. One way of making sure that you do not regress is by using your finger as a visual guide. If your eye is focused on your finger as you read, you will find it impossible to return to previous material without being aware of it. Using your finger as a visual guide will force your eye onwards.

Back-skipping

Back-skipping is similar to regression in that it is a return to material you have previously read. However, unlike regression, it is something that happens unconsciously, like a visual stutter causing your eye to move backwards. This will clearly slow you down and so you should do your best to eliminate it.

The best way to do this is again to use a visual guide, because if your eye is focused on your finger, it will be much more difficult for it to focus on anything else and using a visual guide enables you to control your eye more easily. We discuss using a visual guide in more detail in the upcoming sections.

Inappropriate speed

This problem is simply reading at a speed that is wrong for you. It might be either too fast or too slow. Usually we are taught to slow down for something that we don't understand, yet this may not necessarily be the best solution, as it may lead to a disruption in the rhythm and flow of the material you are reading. In the section on expanding your focus we will show that reading too slowly can be detrimental to comprehension.

Try reading at different speeds: different speeds may be appropriate for different types of material. You may find that you can read contemporary novels more quickly than historical ones because the language is more familiar. Experiment with different speeds to find out what works best for the particular type of material you are reading.

Problems with comprehension

One of the problems you may have is with understanding what you are reading. For instance, you may not be familiar with all of the words in a text. If that is the case, do not pause or stop reading, but carry till the end of the section you are on. The meaning may become clear from the surrounding context. Have a guess as to what you think the word means. There is a good chance you will be right.

Whenever you read, make sure that you have a dictionary readily available. As you read, if you come across any words that you don't understand, make a mark in soft pencil beside them, and when you come to an appropriate break, such as the end of a chapter, use the dictionary to look up the words you have marked.

In the longer term, you should make a continuing effort to expand your vocabulary. As you do this the number of words that you do not recognise or cannot work out will become fewer and fewer.

Concentration

One problem that you might have is an inability to concentrate on what you are reading. You might find that your mind constantly wanders away from the reading material and you find yourself thinking of other things. If this is the case, we suggest you read our Concentration & Focus Quick Course. This will help you with your mental focus and you will be able fully to concentrate on what you are reading without becoming distracted.

Another thing you can do to maintain concentration is to think actively about the material as you read it. Take a critical viewpoint about what is being said: do you agree or disagree with it? What do you think generally about what the author is saying? If you are reading a work of fiction, what do you think about the characters? Do you think the plot is realistic? And so on...

You can also make notes about as you read. The process of note taking ensures that you are much more involved with what you are doing and so helps to maintain concentration.

Motivation

Another factor that may lead to difficulty concentrating is poor motivation. It is difficult to stay focused on something that you are really not interested in. So, if you think that this might be a problem, spend a few minutes brainstorming. Ask yourself why you want to read this particular piece of material. What are your motives? Come up with all of the ultimate benefits that doing so will give you and any intermediate benefits that will accrue.

Also, ask yourself what are the negative consequences if you do not read that material. If you would like to find out more about motivating yourself please see our Goals Quick Course.

If, having brainstormed, you are still not able to come up with any good reasons to read the material, read something else instead!

Onword

Having looked at some of the problems you may have with your reading, in the following section we outline ways of improving your reading habits, ensuring that you are always able to get the most out of your reading in any situation.

TWO

ESTABLISHING GOOD READING HABITS

We have now covered some of the problems that may prevent you from reading at high speeds. Now we will look at some of the things you can do to improve your reading and to make sure that you get the most out of it. The first of these is ensuring that you are in the best state of mind for reading.

State of Mind

If you have read our Concentration & Focus Quick Course you will know that an *alpha* mental state is associated with improved mental performance, and so if you want to read at high speeds you should aim to be in this state whenever you are reading.

Consider for a moment what it actually means to read something. It is much more than merely moving your eyes over the page. Rather, it is a process involving a number of different stages: light particles, or *photons*, hit the page and are reflected towards your eye. They pass through the lens and are focused onto your retina. Here, neurons fire, stimulating the visual cortex. Your brain reorganises the information it receives into visual symbols and recognises these symbols as the letters on the page.

It then builds these symbols up into words and links these words together in a logical fashion, so that you are able comprehend what you are reading.

However, that is not the end of the matter: you still need to store what you read in both short-term and long-term memory to make sense of it, so some form of recall is necessary. This is a highly complicated process involving many different parts of the brain.

It is therefore vitally important that you are in a completely focused state of mind as you read. It will assist you in the initial stages of basic comprehension, with the logical structure of what you are reading and with recall.

Attaining the right state of mind

Sit still for five minutes, and allow yourself to relax. Breathing through your nose, inhale deeply from your abdomen. Breathe in for a count of three, hold for another three count, and exhale for a count of three. Do not strain as you breathe. If you are unsure how to breathe from your abdomen, we examine this in greater detail in our Healthy Breathing Quick Course.

As you sit and breathe, command your mind to be still. Focus entirely on your breath as it goes in and out of your nose. When you have spent five minutes sitting like this, breathing deeply and relaxing, you should be in the right state of mind. Continue breathing slowly and deeply throughout your entire reading session.

Posture

In the long run you will find reading more enjoyable if you adopt a good reading posture. If you slump when you read, your neck and back are bent which will restrict the flow of oxygen to the brain, impeding your mental functioning. So ensure that you keep your back straight when you sit down to read and sit on your sitting bone. Do not strain to adopt a good posture, just be comfortable and well balanced. Use a chair that is both comfortable and conducive to good posture.

Light

You need light to read by and the quality of the light you use can affect the quality and enjoyment of your reading. Natural light is best, so read by sunlight if you can. Try not to read where the sun is too bright or where the shadows and contrast are very strong as this is likely to be distracting. The best options are in the shade or near a window.

If you have to use artificial light make sure that it is not too bright and that it is diffuse, so that there are no sharp shadows. Place the light behind you on your non-writing hand side. Do this particularly if you are going to be writing or marking your book as this will minimise the shadows moving across the page as you read.

If you are reading from a computer screen ensure that you take regular breaks. The screen has a frequency of 50 Hz in the UK and even though you cannot directly perceive this, it may affect you causing headaches and other symptoms.

Avoid reading from a computer before you go to bed. The light from the screen is shifted towards the blue end of the spectrum and this has been shown to disrupt sleep patterns.

Other factors

Other factors that will affect the quality of your reading are those factors that affect intellectual performance as a whole. These include your levels of overall fitness, especially cardiovascular fitness and muscular flexibility, as well as the quality of your diet and the quality of your nutrition. If you are truly committed to ensuring that you brain performs as well as it possibly can, you should consider looking at each of these areas as well.

Onword

We have now been through a number of factors that will help you become a better reader and make your reading more enjoyable. In part two, we focus specifically on speed reading, showing you how to read at speeds of up to 1,000 wpm.

PART 2

READING AT UP TO 1,000 WPM

FOUR

READING FASTER – UP TO 1,000 WPM

In this section you will build on the good practice you have established in part one and develop your skills for reading at speed. The aim of this section is to show you specifically how to read at up to 1,000 words per minute. For many people this will be sufficient.

To read at 1,000 wpm you will be reading 'normally' – that is, more or less how you read at the moment but faster and more efficiently. The techniques for reading at speeds higher than 1,000 wpm are slightly different and we will outline those in part three.

Here, we will look at how the eye moves when you are reading and use this knowledge to outline some basic skills you should use when you read. As with any skill, it will not be something you master immediately, but by adopting the right strategies you will be reading much more quickly in a very short space of time.

We are going to ask you to do a number of reading exercises. Some of these use material contained within the course itself. For others you will need a book of your own. We suggest that you choose this book now.

Ideally, use a novel. Don't use one that has difficult language or a very small font. Make it a light, easy reading novel. Use one that you have not read before, but that perhaps is by an author you are familiar with so that you know the level of difficulty.

We want to train your eye without overloading your brain. If you use a book containing difficult material, a larger proportion of your brain's processing power will be used for comprehending it. At present simply concern yourself with reading more quickly. When you can do this with easy reading, you can then move on to more difficult material.

It is important whenever you are reading that you are not self-conscious as this will take you out of the concentrated and focused state of mind you need to read effectively. Some of the exercises we are going to do may, initially at least, take you out of that zone because of their newness. As such it is important that you make sure you practise them. One of the aims of practising is to ensure that the new techniques you adopt are not a distraction but be aware that in the early days they may be.

Establishing your current reading speed

So that you know what improvements in reading speed you make you should gain an idea of how fast you currently read. To do this, first we are going to make a few simple calculations using the book you have chosen.

Open your book to a page within the main text and count how many words there are on four full lines: that is lines that don't stop part way through such as happens at the end of a paragraph. Divide the number you get by four.

This will give you the average number of words on a line. It doesn't need to be exact. For most novels this will be in the range of eight to twelve words although some might have more, some fewer. Make a note of this number. You will need it for later in this section and in subsequent exercises.

Now count up the number of lines on a page. This should be a page full of text, so not the first or last page of a chapter. For most novels this will be between thirty-five and fifty lines. Again some may have fewer, some more.

Multiply the two numbers you have ascertained together. This will provide you with the average number of words on a full page of text. Of course the precise number of words on a page will vary from page to page. This number will, however, be precise enough for our purposes.

If you recorded an average of twelve words on a line and thirty-five lines on a page this would give you a total of 420 words on a page.

Now, set yourself up in a comfortable reading environment, take your book and simply read as you normally would for five minutes. Do not try to read faster or slower than normal. Simply read in a relaxed, comfortable, unselfconscious manner. Use a timer with an audible alarm that will notify you when five minutes have elapsed. This way you will not have to keep glancing at your watch. Make a note of where you start reading from.

When the five minutes are up count how many pages you have read. If a page was only half full of text count this as half a page. If a page had a picture which took up one-third of a page with the remaining two-thirds as text, count this as two thirds. You want to know how many pages of full text you have read.

Suppose that after five minutes you have read four full pages of text. Multiply the number of pages read, four, by the number of words on a page – in our example, 420. This will give you the total number of words you have read: 1,680.

Finally, divide this number by five (the number of minutes for which you have been reading) to give you the number of words you normally read in a minute: 336.

You can now measure exactly how much faster you read as you progress through the course. Be aware that you will read at different speeds for different kinds of material. A difficult academic text will take longer to read than a novel by Dan Brown. However, as you progress with your speed reading training you will find that you are able to read all types of material more quickly. You will probably find that you still read difficult material more slowly than easy material.

Comprehension

Considering the passage you have just read, score yourself on a scale of 1 to 10 for comprehension. Again this is to give you a baseline as you practise. If you have followed our suggestion you have just read an easy novel for five minutes at your normal reading speed. Your comprehension, therefore, should be as high as it is likely to be under any circumstances.

Score yourself out of ten. If you think you understood it perfectly, score ten. If you understand not one word of it, then give yourself a score of one. Hopefully, your score will be nearer ten than one for this exercise.

Whenever we ask you to do an exercise using your own book remember as well as measuring your reading speed to score your comprehension too. There is little point being able to read at very high speeds if you don't understand a word of what you have read.

Onword

Now that you know how fast you normally read, we are going to introduce the factors that will help you to read faster, starting with the use of a visual guide.

FIVE

USING A VISUAL GUIDE

We have already shown that it is easier to focus your eye exactly where you want to by using a visual guide. Using a guide means that you will be able to ensure your eye stops at the desired point on the page, rather than at random haphazard intervals. You can use either your finger, most likely your index finger, or a pen as your guide. We suggest that if possible you use a pen. This places less strain on the muscles in the wrist and obscures less text than if you use your finger.

Please take your novel and read it for five minutes using your pen as a visual guide. Move the point of your pen (or finger) underneath the line you are reading in a smooth motion from the first word of the line to the last word and then down to the beginning of the next line and so on. Keep your eye focused on the tip of the pen as you read.

Maintain a constant speed that is comfortable for you to read at. Do not try at this stage to go faster or slower than you normally do. Move the guide at a natural speed.

Make a note of your starting and finishing points and calculate your speed in words per minute and your level of comprehension as before. Your reading speed may have gone up or down, as may your comprehension.

If your speed has gone down do not worry. The point of this exercise is simply to introduce you to using a visual guide. You can move a pen under a line of text as slowly or as quickly as you like so if you want to read faster, simply move the pen faster keeping your eye on the tip.

As for your comprehension, some people find that it helps immediately. Others may be a little distracted by the introduction of the visual guide and find that comprehension goes down. As you continue to use a guide this distraction will gradually diminish.

Unless we specifically say not to, use a visual guide for all the reading exercises in this course and try to use one for your everyday reading. If you find that you are unable to use a guide when reading normally, attempt to move your eyes in the same pattern. Using a visual guide so that your eye can be properly directed is one of the essential elements to reading at higher speeds.

Eye movements

Try the following exercise before reading any further. Find someone who is willing to be a guinea pig and have them read a book for a page or two. Sit opposite them a couple of feet away and notice how their eyes move. If you cannot see their eyes easily, move closer or ask them to raise their head until you can. Watch them as closely as possible. Do this before you read on.

What you will have observed, possibly contrary to your expectations, is that their eyes did not move smoothly. If you watched closely you will have seen them moving along the line in a series of small jumps from left to right – or right to left from your perspective - and then a big jump when they reached the end of the line and started reading the line below.

These eye movements are called saccadic eye movements and one movement is called a saccade. Take a moment to contemplate why the eyes might move this way and not smoothly as you may have expected.

Most people when asked this respond that the visual system takes in more than one word at a time. While this is true - we do see more than one word at a time - this does not explain why it is necessary for the eyes to pause.

The real reason is simply that to take in information off a page of text the eye must be still in relation to that text. If it is moving the text will be blurry and so no information will be taken in.

Try this exercise. Hold your index finger up in front of you at your normal reading distance. Hold this page immediately behind it so that it is touching your finger. Focus your eyes on your finger. Now, keeping your finger still and your eyes focused there, move the page behind it around in a circle. If you do this correctly you will notice that all the text goes out of focus.

Now remove your finger and focus your eyes on a word in the middle of the page. Move the page around in a circle as before. You will find that your eye naturally picks out a point on the page and follows it around. This time the text will be in focus.

This exercise shows that your eye needs to be still in relation to the text that it is looking at to be able to see it properly. If it is moving in relation to that text, it will be out of focus.

So, when you are reading, your eye must stop temporarily to focus on each word or group of words. Each such stop is called a fixation. The eye is capable of making between three and five of these fixations per second.

The average length of a fixation is 200-250 ms (thousandths of a second). The eye takes between 20-40 ms to move from one point of fixation to the next and the average distance between each fixation is seven to nine characters. This information can help us to read more quickly.

Implications for speed

The implications for reading at higher speeds are straightforward. In order to speed up your reading, you need either to increase the number of fixations per second by moving your eyes more quickly, or alternatively, increase the distance between fixations by taking in more words with every fixation.

One way of reading at about 1,000 wpm would be to make four fixations per second and take in four words per fixation (sixteen words a second). Alternatively, you could read at three fixations per second but take in a slightly higher number of words each time, say five (fifteen words a second).

The following sections will help you to establish the number of fixations per second you are capable of making and to raise that number. They will also help you to increase the number of words you can take in on each fixation.

Increasing the number of words per fixation will ultimately be more useful than moving your eyes more quickly as there is a limit to how quickly you can comfortably move your eyes. Also, the receptors in your retina can only fire about five times a second so more than five fixations per second would not enable you to take in any more information.

Basic exercises

Having explained what is necessary to speed up your reading, we are going to outline exactly how to go about it. We will look at: -

- Increasing the number of fixations per second your eyes can make;
- Strengthening the eye muscles;
- Expanding your focus;
- Showing where to focus by using your visual guide.

Onword

In the following section we will look in more detail at taking control of your eye movement, establishing a constant rhythm and increasing the number of fixations per second that you can make.

SIX

CONTROLLING EYE MOVEMENT

The aim of this section is to establish how many individual fixations your eye can make in a second and to push that number as high as you can.

To do this you are going to need a way of measuring the number of movements your eye can make in a second. We suggest that you use a metronome.

A metronome is a device that sounds out a beat and which you can adjust to whatever speed you choose. Usually, they are used to keep a beat when playing a musical instrument. However, we are going to use one to help you read more quickly.

If you don't have a physical metronome you can use one either online or download one as an app. We suggest that you do this now as you will need it for the upcoming exercise.

When you have one that you are happy with, make sure that you know how to use it and how to adjust the settings so that you can control the number of beats in a second. Make sure that you can sound out 2, 2.5, 3, 3.5, 4, 4.5 beats per second (bps).

If you cannot gain access to any sort of metronome use the second hand of a clock or watch instead.

On the following page you will see a whole page with dots marked upon it.

Your aim is to move your eyes from one dot to the next, focusing on each one, going along the page from left to right and then down a line in the same way as you do when you are reading. Each movement should be to the beat established by the metronome: one fixation per beat. One dot per beat.

Initially, set the metronome to two beats per second and move your eye from dot to dot until you have completed the page.

When you have done so, increase the fixation rate to 2.5 beats per second and repeat the exercise. Keep on increasing the speed by half a beat per second until you reach a speed that feels uncomfortably fast. Make sure that you are moving your eyes and not your head. When we read we do not generally move our heads, only our eyes.

Make a note of the fastest beat that you are comfortable with. This fixation rate will be the rate that you are going to use in the remaining exercises. So if you could comfortably focus three times per second, use a metronome beating at three beats per second in the following exercises and whenever we ask you to use a metronome.

Initially do this exercise without a visual guide. When you have reached the highest speed that you can reach without a guide, repeat the process with a guide.

You can do this in one of two ways and we suggest that you try both. You can move your guide at a constant speed in the same way as you did previously. Alternatively, you could move the guide from dot to dot on the beat resting it for a moment on each dot before moving onto the next one. This mirrors the saccadic movements that your eyes make. You should practise this second technique as you will need it for subsequent exercises.

You will probably find that you can make more fixations per second using a guide than without one.

If, at the end of this exercise, you find that your eyes are a little tired, take a short break. Also, if you find that reading at your fastest fixation rate for an extended period tires your eyes out too much, slow down just a little. But, as your eye muscles get stronger, try not to do this.

As time progresses and as you find your eye muscles getting stronger, aim to increase your number of fixations per second but keep good form and ensure that your point of focus is always under control.

Your fixation rate need not be a whole number. If you find that four fixations per second is manageable while five is beyond you, try four and a half instead. Always try to go as fast as you can, while at the same time keeping good form. Keep repeating this exercise regularly to push your eyes to move and focus more quickly.

As we stated earlier, there is a limit to the number of fixations you can make in a second. For our purposes, if you can manage three fixations a second you will be able, with practice, to read at 1,000 wpm.

Strengthening the Eye

In order for the eye to accurately stop, focus, move on, stop, focus and move on again, the muscles of the eye need to be in good condition. If you are making three fixations per second, in one hour of reading your eye will make 10,800 individual movements. As with any other muscles, the muscles that control your eyes can get tired.

Below we set out a number of exercises that will strengthen the muscles of the eye. We suggest that you conduct these exercises every day as part of your reading practice.

Exercise 1

Centre your head and focus your eyes straight in front of you. Now, keeping your head still and moving only your eyes, look up as far as you can. Keep the movement slow. It should take about one second to complete. Hold your eyes at the top for a second and move them back to the centre again. Now look down, hold and return to the centre in exactly the same way. Do this sequence five times. Remember to breathe slowly through the nose.

Now do the same, looking to the left and returning to the centre and then to the right, moving your eyes as far as you can each time. When you have done that move your eyes diagonally up-left and down-right and then down-left and up-right centring them between each movement and completing each sequence five times.

Unless you have exercised your eye muscles before, you might find this quite tiring. As they get stronger slow down each movement that you make. This will make your eye muscles work harder. Each movement and each hold should be one second long when you start doing these exercises but aim to extend that to five seconds as your eyes get stronger.

Exercise 2

Centre your head and eyes again. Keeping your head still, look up as far as you can and then slowly move your eyes in a circle, starting at the top and moving clockwise. Make the circle as large as it can possibly be. This will stretch your eye muscles. Keep the movement slow and steady. Do this five times. Then do the same moving your eyes in an anti-clockwise direction. Again, as your eyes get stronger, slow down your eye movement to work the muscles harder.

Exercise 3

Centre your head and your eyes. Find an object directly in front of you that is a long way away and focus on it. It could be a spot on a far wall or something you can see outside through a window. You may need to change the direction you are facing to do this.

Now hold your finger up in front of you, and keeping it in focus, move it slowly towards your eyes. Stop moving it just before it starts to go out of focus. Your finger should be at the closest point that you can focus on.

You are now ready to start the exercise. Holding your finger in place, switch your focus between your finger and the distant object ten times in succession, focusing on each object for one second. As your eye gets stronger, see if you can move your finger closer to your face and still keep it in focus, and increase the number of repetitions from ten to twenty.

Over time, these exercises should strengthen your eye muscles, enabling you to read for longer without getting eye strain or headaches and ensuring that you can control exactly where your eye focuses as well as helping you to raise your fixation rate.

Onword

In the following section we examine the second element vital to speeding up your reading: increasing the number of words that you can take in on each fixation.

SEVEN

EXPANDING YOUR FOCUS

Eye physiology

By using a device called a tachistoscope, which flashes words on a screen for a short space of time, it has been shown that the eye is capable of seeing as many as four words in just two one-thousandths of a second. This means that in one second it can recognise as many as two thousand words, or about seven pages of an average book. It is our aim to get you reading at about 1,000 words a minute, one hundredth of that speed, so you can see that your eye is certainly up to the task.

The inside surface of your eye, the retina, contains about 130 million light sensitive cells, each of which responds to the colour and intensity of light. Each cell is capable of processing about five photons every second. Your perception is sharpest at an area of the retina called the fovea. This area is very small: it occupies about 1/40,000 of your visual field. This corresponds to about three letters at a distance of two feet.

Try this now: hold your book about two feet from your eye, and focus on any word. You should find that about three letters stand out in sharp focus while all the others are peripheral. However, the fact that a word is in your peripheral vision does not prevent you from reading it. Try focusing on the word you just looked at. Without moving your eyes, you should still be able to recognise words close to the one you are looking at.

In fact it may not appear that any of the words nearby are out of focus at all. This is not because of your eye but because of your brain. Your brain is capable of correcting the deficiencies in your vision making it look as if what you see in your peripheral vision is in good focus.

This is what your eye actually sees: -

As you can see by looking at the blurry line, you only see the word 'four' perfectly. The words on either side become more blurry the further away you get so that more than two or three words away on either side it is very blurry indeed, nearly too blurry to make sense of.

Yet focus on the other 'four' in the line above and you will notice that the whole line appears more or less in focus. This is because of the amazing processing power of your brain. Your brain is capable of correcting the blurred information it receives via the eye and converting it into something that makes sense.

Thus you can read without focusing sharply on every word. In fact, doing so slows you down and feels unnatural. We will make use of this knowledge in the following set of exercises on expanding your focus.

Expanding your focus

We stated earlier that there are essentially two ways of speeding up your reading: either increasing the number of fixations per second your eye makes (the speed your eye moves), or increasing the number of words you take in on each fixation.

You may intuitively suppose that you take in one word on every fixation but a moment's thought will reveal that that is not the case. When earlier on you observed your partners eyes moving as they read, they made about four or five fixations per line. This is fewer than the number of words on a line and thus it must be the case that more than one word is taken in one each fixation.

In fact we can take in a number of words at a time. When we first learnt to read as children (depending on the method we were taught to read) we learnt the sound of each letter and built those sounds up into words. Once we become fluent we could read one whole word at a time. However, there is no reason to stop there. In fact without any further training at all, we naturally read more than one word on each fixation and in fact reading just one word at a time feels unnaturally slow.

To see this, read the following passage, an extract from the opening of Peter Pan. Each word has been placed separately on the page, and so your eye is forced to read just one word at a time.

All	children,	except
one,	grow	up.
They	soon	know
that	they	will
grow	up,	and
the	way	Wendy
knew	was	this.
One	day	when
she	was	two
years	old	she
was	playing	in
a	garden,	and
she	plucked	another
flower	and	ran
with	it	to
her	mother.	I
suppose	she	must
have	looked	rather
delightful,	for	Mrs
Darling	put	her
hand	to	her

heart and cried, 'Oh, why can't you remain like this forever!'

This was all that passed between them on the subject, but henceforth Wendy knew that she must grow up.

You always know after you are two.

Two is the beginning of the end.

Of course they lived at 14,

(their	house	number
on	their	street)
and	until	Wendy
came	her	mother
was	the	chief
one.	She	was
a	lovely	lady,
with	a	romantic
mind	and	such
a	sweet	mocking
mouth.		

For most people this passage feels unnatural and stilted. Taking in one word at a time slows you down, restricts the amount of information you take in with each eye fixation and prevents you from grouping words into concepts.

The eye can take in a number of words in one go and to read at high speeds you should take advantage of this fact. Furthermore, it doesn't matter if in doing this you do not take in every word you read. It is possible to leave out some words and still be able to understand what you are reading.

We are now going to see how many words at a time your eye can comfortably take in. Over the following pages are a number of word sequences. Your aim is to take in the whole sequence in just one fixation. You will start off with shorter sequences and then move on to longer ones. The first page has sequences of just two words, the page after that three words, then four and so on.

Set your metronome to the fixation rate you have previously identified. Find a piece of card or a blank sheet of paper. Turn to the first pair of words and cover them up with the card. Then, in time with the metronome, move the card out of the way so that you can see the sequence, and then replace it, covering up the sequence once again. Reveal the word sequence for one beat of the metronome only.

Your aim is to make sure that you are able to see and read both words in the time available. Ask yourself whether you are able to see the words and make a mental check that you understood them before moving on to the next pair.

As you work through the exercise the sequences get longer. Push yourself so that you take in ever more words per fixation. Make a note of the maximum number of words that you can take in at any one time and the next time you practise try to go one higher.

2 words

long ago

drink me

every day

keen sense

greater part

correct time

always caught

friendly circle

fine afternoon

swallow-tailed

because nothing

invariably stood

extremely funny

murmuring crowd

hideous instrument

sometimes happens

consternation pierced

mysterious Englishmen

aforementioned gentleman

3 words

I was born

He smote the

had slept well

observed in this

settle in London

sweat and sweat

could not prevail

rustics and hinds

two elder brothers

were in tantrums

black curling hair

holding our hearts

Holmes was sitting

should always find

beauty every region

labour and suffering

days of photographs

excellent counsel against

most affectionate manner

4 words

look in the eyes

on their own land

We can't do much

It was enough for

I was well enough

lad of about fifteen

the wolves of India

another form of life

saucily to the world

but she had departed

have been very happy

They were fresh, blond

came and went without

from joining the group

how they are transfused

had lived for generations

The women were different

lying hard and unresponsive

Perhaps no district throughout

5 words

I was going to tell

and when fit to go

The little girl will be

in most of which her

are not so many men

turn and plant of each

I hate the way you talk

so much for her person

there is really very little

but I really can't exhibit

As the painter looked at

voice was very stern now

I am all expectation, Basil

washing dishes at the sink

that noble mole is washed

Polly hesitated, then went on

to extend a gracious reception

the mourning draperies of cloud

innocent people may suffer, hereafter

6 words

They live in a valley of

The first place that I can

even if he had, they were

who had noticed the tone of

The day broke gray and dull.

And the bottles come in here

with a threatening shake of his

That constant pacing to and fro

The sullen murmur of the bees

shop window is often better for

genius for knowing when a cough

Then followed the history and rise

and thinking it always desirable for

A wide plain, where the broadening

might reasonably be explained by the

Wherein the tongued consuls can propose

concise and faithful specimen of biography

dragging along in turbulent confusion behind

Sorelli was very superstitious. She shuddered

The purpose of this exercise is to increase the number of words you can take in. Make a note of this number.

You will need to keep practising to expand your focus, so you will either need to print out word sequences of your own or alternatively you could make use of certain websites or apps which enable you to do the same. One suggested app is quickreader and a suitable website is spreeder.com. We will say a little more about these later when we talk about practicing your speed reading skills.

Applying these skills to reading

You now know how many fixations per second your eye can make and how many words you can take in at any one time. We are now going to use this information to speed up your reading.

First we are going to use the number of words you recorded in the exercise you have just done. Let us suppose that you could read four words at a time but struggled with five. Whenever you are reading, you would want to take in four words on every fixation.

Consider the following sequence of four words:

have been very happy

It should be apparent that the place to focus on so that you can see the whole sequence in one go is in the middle, here marked by **X**:

have been**X**very happy

So when reading, ideally you would find the middle of one sequence of four words, and focusing there, read those four words. You would then move on to the next set of four words, find the middle of that sequence, read those four and so on. The phrase,

The fool has had no more sense than to jump at a

would become: -

[The fool has had] [no more sense than] [to jump at a]

Your points of focus would be the 'l' of fool, the 's' of sense and the 'p' of jump.

However there is clearly a practical problem with this. In order to read each set of four words, you would have to count forward four words, find the mid-point, focus on that point and from that point read the four surrounding words.

Clearly this is not an appropriate method as it would take time to count each set of four words and find the middle – by that time it would not be worth focusing because you would have already seen all the words that you were planning to read, and it would terribly disrupt the flow of your reading. Accordingly, we will not be using this approach.

However, we want to try to ensure that you obtain the same amount of information on every fixation that your eye makes. So, we suggest the following approach. Rather than count words, divide up each line of text into sections.

When you calculated your current reading speed, we asked you to make a note of the average number of words on a line. Let us suppose that you calculated that there were twelve words per line on average. You would simply divide the each line into three equal sections (because you read four words at a time) and your points of focus would be the middle of those sections. On average you would be reading four words on each fixation. Since the number of words on each line is just an average, sometimes you would take in slightly more than four, others slightly fewer.

A twelve word line would have the following points of focus:

[The fool hXas had no][more senseX than to j][ump at a Xwoodcutter']

The advantage of using this approach is that you can use the same points of focus on each and every line, establishing a kind of rhythm of place for your eyes to move to. For example, for a twelve word line divided into groups of four words, you would focus on the following points.

X	X	X
X	X	X
X	X	X

With a twelve word line divided into groups of three words, you would focus on the following points:

X	X	X	X
X	X	X	X
X	X	X	X

If you book had fifteen words a line and you could read at three words at a time your points of focus would be:

X	X	X	X	X
X	X	X	X	X
X	X	X	X	X

Each point is equidistant from each other and your eyes simply move from one point of focus to the next, moving along the line and then down to the next line.

We now suggest that you take your novel and do the following exercise. The purpose of this exercise is to get you used to moving your eye to the right points on the page so that you can take in the correct number of words each time.

For ease of demonstration we have used an example that makes the maths easy. A line with twelve words divides by four words to give a whole number of fixations, three.

If the book you are using has a number of words per line that does not divide easily, simply use either of the nearest approximations. For example, suppose you found that your book has thirteen words in a line and you are able to read five words at a time. Five doesn't divide into thirteen a whole number of times.

Five goes into thirteen 2.6 times. So instead either divide your line into two, or divide it into three. Dividing it into two would mean that you are reading slightly more words on average than you are comfortable with (6.5 words), dividing into three would mean slightly fewer words (4.3 words). So dividing the line into three would be a little easier.

Using your novel, work out how you are going to divide up each line you read and ensure that you know where your points of fixation will be on each line.

As before, read for five minutes making a note of your starting and finishing points. Record the number of words you have read and your comprehension score as before. The first time you do this, the aim is simply to get you accustomed to reading at your desired number of words per fixation. As you repeat the exercise over time, aim to do it more quickly.

Use your pen as visual guide but for the moment do not use the metronome. Rather than moving the pen smoothly however, move it in jumps, one from one point of fixation to the next.

At this stage do not use the metronome.

When you have done this exercise using a visual guide, repeat it without one. You will not always be able to use a visual guide when reading, so it is important to train your eyes naturally to go to the desired point of fixation.

One point that you may have noticed is that when you use this approach you do not directly look at the first or the last words on any line. They are seen only in peripheral vision. This may take a little getting used to.

If you haven't used a visual guide before, remember that when practising a new skill that requires concentration, people have a tendency to tense their bodies and to hold their breath, so be aware of this and stay as physically relaxed as you can. Keep your breathing slow and measured, and your body, especially your guide hand and shoulders, relaxed.

You will have noticed as you read that not all lines are filled with text. Often where there is speech only the left-hand side of the page has text on it. Also, when a paragraph ends, the last line may be shorter.

This line stops at the halfway point.

The right hand side of the line above is blank. When reading using your guide, you can save yourself time by skipping over any blank areas.

Combining the faster reading skills

You are now going to combine what we have covered in this section with what we discussed in the previous one. You are going to repeat the last exercise, but this time with the metronome switched on. You will move from one point of fixation to the next on each beat of the metronome.

If performed properly, this exercise will get you reading at or near your current potential maximum reading speed. You will be taking in as many words on each fixation as you are comfortable with, and you will be moving your eyes at the highest speed you currently can.

Suppose you can read at three beats of the metronome a second and you can take in four words on each fixation. You should be reading at twelve words per second or 720 words per minute.

As before do this reading exercise using your novel, reading for five minutes and recording your actual speed and comprehension.

It is very likely that the first time you do this exercise your comprehension will fall significantly. You are pushing yourself to your maximum current potential speed. While it is fairly easy to see one set of four words in a third of a second, seeing four words three times a second for five minutes is harder and will initially be difficult to cope with. This is why you will need to practise. We set out how in subsequent chapters.

One thing we have observed when people do this exercise is that, because they are moving quite fast across the page, they instinctively slow down, and this happens by 'losing' the beat of the metronome. Rather than making one fixation per beat, they make one fixation every second beat for example. So we suggest that before you start reading, you simply tap your pen (or finger) along with the beat. Once you are happy that you are moving it to the beat, start reading.

When you have finished, record your speed. It should be higher than previously. And record your comprehension. It may well have gone down for the moment.

Onword

Make sure that you understand this section fully before you move on. Ensure that you know how many words you can comfortably take in on each fixation.

Check that you understand why it is important to divide each line of any text you are reading into sections. Check that you know how to divide up the line, depending on the number of words you can take in and the average number of words per line. For different books with different numbers of words on a line, you may have to divide up the lines differently.

The final exercise may have resulted in a drop in comprehension. In the following two sections we discuss how to apply what you have learnt to help you read more quickly and to ensure that your comprehension remains high.

EIGHT

READING FASTER: PRACTICE 1

Basic Practice

So far, we have covered the use of a visual guide, moving your eyes at a particular pace and expanding your focus by increasing the number of words you take in at a time.

You should practise all of these elements until they become second nature. We outline how below.

Using a visual guide

Practise regularly using a visual guide until you get used to it. Use either a pen or your finger. As we have mentioned a pen is preferable as it obscures less text and places less strain on your wrist. Try to do all of your reading with a visual guide if you can. In situations where you cannot, move your eyes in the same pattern as you would if you were.

Set aside some time specifically to practise using a guide until it becomes second nature. You might start by moving your guide smoothly along each line of text until your eye is accustomed to following it. Do this for one chapter or your novel every day if you can.

You should also practise moving your guide from point to point. In the previous section you calculated the points of focus on each line for the novel you are using. Practise using your guide this way for at least one chapter per day.

Finally practise moving your eyes in exactly the same manner - from one point of fixation to the next - but without using your guide. This will enable you to move your eyes to the appropriate points in situations where you are unable to use your guide.

Do this for one chapter a day. Do each of these exercises without the metronome. Here you are focusing purely on using your guide. Do, however, make a note of your speed and comprehension.

Use of a metronome

Use your metronome to ensure that you move your eyes to a smooth rhythm. If you want, you can use the page filled with dots as practice. Do this both with and without a visual guide.

We suggest that you use a metronome only when practising. You won't want to use one when reading for real. However, if you want to have a rhythm to read to when you are reading normally, you can use music. We suggest instrumental music rather than songs, as lyrics can be distracting. However, ultimately use music you like to listen to.

As you practise moving your eyes more quickly, you might also want to incorporate the eye exercises we have outlined. Over time, this will ensure that your eyes do not get over-tired.

Increasing words per fixation

Use exercises similar to those you did earlier to increase the number of words that you take in on one fixation. You may have to create sequences of words yourself and print them off.

Alternatively there are websites that you can use that fulfil the same function. For example, see www.spreeder.com. With spreeder.com a text window appears in the middle of the screen and an amount of text can be pasted into that window.

When started, the window will flash up so many words at a time in the same area of the window. You can adjust this in settings where it says chunk size. Aim to increase the word count up to 5 or 6 words at a time. Ensure the font size is such that all the words appear on one line (e.g. font size 14 or lower). Adjust the words per minute so that a new sequence of words flashes up three or four times a second (or however many fixations you can comfortably make in a second). You should be able to read a little faster with this application because the words you are reading flash up in the same place. You do not have to move your eyes.

Alternatively there are various apps that you download. We like the Quick Reader app which highlights the words you should be focusing on. It allows you to set a particular reading speed and an appropriate number of fixations per line.

Comprehension

Remember when reading that as you get faster it is important to assess your comprehension. As we mentioned you can give yourself a score out of ten for each chapter. This is a subjective score. If you would like a more objective measure of your comprehension, you could try the following.

When you come to the end of an exercise, write a summary of what you have read. Firstly, do it after having read a chapter at normal speed. This will give you an idea of how much information you usually take in.

Then when you have done a speed-reading exercise write another summary. If you find that this summary is less detailed, it might mean that you are taking less in – even if you are not aware of it. You can use this approach to comprehension for the exercises in the following chapter.

Onword

In the following section we look at more ways to practise, this time aimed specifically at helping you attain speeds of up to 1,000 wpm.

NINE

READING FASTER: PRACTICE 2

Reading at 1,000 wpm

Now that you are familiar with the basic speed reading skills we are going to show you specifically how to practise to get up to 1,000 wpm.

You are going to use your novel. The practice regime we suggest will take about half an hour to complete. It consists of six stages each lasting five minutes.

For each stage you will be using the metronome. We suggest that you use a beat of three beats a second. If you are happy using a higher rate then feel free to do so. However, to read at 1,000 wpm three beats a second will be sufficient.

We are also going to assume that the book you are using contains twelve words a line on average. If you are using a book with a different number of words, adjust our advice as necessary.

Stage 1

Divide each line into four. This means that you should be reading three words at a time on average. Use your pen as a visual guide and read for five minutes at this rate. This should be relatively easy for you. If it is too much, divide the line into five instead. When you have finished, score your comprehension out of ten and if you have sufficient time write a summary of what you have read as suggested in the previous section.

If you do this precisely, you should be reading at a speed of 9 words a second (3 beats a second taking in 3 words each time) or 540 words a minute.

Stage 2

This stage is exactly the same as stage 1, except that you will divide each line into three sections rather than four. Everything else remains the same. If you do this, you should be reading slightly faster (3 beats a second taking in 4 words each time). This time you will be reading at about 720 words a minute. Again, record your actual reading speed and your comprehension score, writing a summary if you have time.

Stage 3

This stage is the same as stage 2, except this time you will divide each line into two sections. Everything else remains the same. If you do this, you should be reading faster still (3 beats a second taking in 6 words each time). Now you will be reading at about 1,080 words a minute. This is roughly our target speed. Again note your actual speed and make sure that you note your levels of comprehension.

Stage 4

This stage is the same as stage 3, except this time you don't divide the line at all, leaving it as one complete section. In other words your eye will be focusing on the centre of each line, going down the page vertically, one line on each beat.

If you do this, you will be reading faster still (3 beats a second taking in 12 words each time). You will be reading at about 2,160 words a minute. The reason for this is to go faster than your eye / brain system can cope with.

This stage uses the so-called motorway effect, which is analogous to when you have spent some time driving at a high speed and then have to slow down.

Often, when doing this you underestimate how fast you are going. For instance, imagine you have been driving on a motorway at 70 mph for some time. You then exit the motorway and come into a town with a limit of 30 mph. You might think you are doing 30 mph when in fact you are doing 50 mph. In other words, you are going faster than you think you are.

Similarly, by forcing yourself to read at a very high speed, of 2,000 wpm and then slowing down, you will find your natural reading speed is now much faster.

Having done this move on to stage 5.

Stage 5

This stage is exactly the same as stage 3. You will again divide each line into two sections. Again you should be reading at about 1080 wpm. However, this time you are slowing down to your desired speed rather than speeding up to it. You should therefore find it easier. Record your actual speed and comprehension as before.

Stage 6

Spend five minutes reading normally, but pushing yourself to read faster. Switch off the metronome but use music if you want to. Use your visual guide. Record your reading speed and comprehension. You should find this speed rising over time.

What you might experience

If you want to read at 1,000 wpm it will not happen overnight. We suggest that you practise as suggested for 30 minutes every day. Over the course of a few weeks, you will find that your reading speed increases significantly.

The first few times you do this exercise you might find stages 3,4 & 5 confusing and feel that you are taking in very little information, if any at all. When you are reading at 1,000 wpm you may initially only pick out a few words and get a vague gist of what is going on.

However, over time you will find that you start to take in more and more. This will happen as your brain starts to get used to these higher speeds. As you read faster, you are taking in more information. Since you probably have not done any specific reading training since school, you will have become accustomed to taking in information at a certain rate.

By pushing yourself faster, you will be forcing yourself to do something that you brain is not used to. Over time, it will become accustomed to these higher speeds, however.

Training your eyes to move to the correct places on the page is the relatively easy part. These eye movement strategies are all designed to ensure that your brain receives more information in a given time. The purpose of these practice exercises is to accustom your brain to receiving these larger amounts of information.

As you do all of these exercises, make sure that you are as relaxed, concentrated and focused as you can be. If you haven't already read them, our quick courses on Concentration & Focus and Healthy Breathing will help.

Once you feel that you have mastered this approach you can move onto the next section which deals with reading even faster. Alternatively, if you need to read material that is more complex than the novel that you have been using so far, you might like to practise using a more difficult book.

Onword

This completes the sections aimed at helping you read at 1,000 wpm. In part three, we set out how to read even faster, at speeds of 2,000, 3,000 or 4,000 wpm. Do not try these until you are happy reading at 1,000 wpm.

PART 3

READING FASTER THAN 1,000 WPM

TEN

READING AT 2,000 WPM

The 1,000 wpm limit

We have stated that 1,000 wpm is the limit for normal reading. Why is this? We can find out if we take another look at the diagram below. As you can see, the further and further away the text is from the word 'four', the more blurred it is.

We can only really see two words on either side before it becomes too blurry to see easily – five words in total. This is no problem for reading at 1,000 wpm. Remember this requires us only to take in between five and six words on each fixation. If we want to read at 2,000 wpm, it follows we have to take in 10-12 words on each fixation.

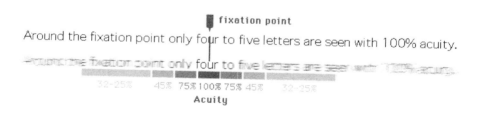

We have so far been considering a normal novel with 12 words a line. We can read at 1,000 wpm by taking in two fixations on each line. If we want to read faster then, it follows that the only way to do so is with one fixation per line. It is impossible to have fractions of a fixation. You cannot have 1.5 fixations or 1.75 fixations per line. These would simply amount to a second fixation.

The only way to have fewer than two fixations and thereby take in more words on each fixation is to have just one fixation per line. And if you have just one, if follows that the only sensible place to use as your point of focus is the middle of the line. But as we have just seen, when we do this the words at the periphery are too blurry.

So in that case, how can we possibly read faster? One way would be to increase the speed of our eye movements, increasing the rate of the metronome. However, as we have seen the fastest we can take in separate images is about five per second. Also, not many people can comfortably move their eyes significantly faster than 3 bps.

This would seem to rule out both possibilities and therefore mean that we cannot read any faster.

However, there is one further possibility that we have not considered. Although our eyes can only see about two words on either side of our point of focus with reasonably clarity, they can also see the same distance above and below the point of fixation. We are going to use that fact to take in information not just from the line we are reading but also from the line below at the same time.

Consider the following passage:

Four score and seven years **X**ago our fathers brought forth

on this continent a new n**X**ation, conceived in Liberty,

and dedicated to the propositio**X**n that all men are created equal

To read at 2,000 wpm (using a beat of 3 bps), the points of fixation would be where the **X**'s are, but as we have seen the words at the beginning of the three lines – four, on, and – and the words at the end - forth, liberty, equal – will be very blurry.

However, if the lines were rearranged like this, again using the **X** as your point of focus, all the words are now easily within range of your fixation point: -

Four score and
seven yea**X**rs ago our
fathers brought forth

on this continent
a new **X**nation,
conceived in Liberty,

and dedicated to
the propo**X**sition that
all men are created equal

Now, no words are very far from the fixation point and they are therefore all in reasonable focus. If all the reading we ever did were arranged like this, then it would be possible to read at higher speeds much more easily.

Unfortunately, this is not the case for most books. This technique can however be used when reading newspapers, where there may only be four or five words in every column. You could read one set of three lines, then move your point of focus down three lines and then take in the subsequent set of three lines.

The same approach can be used for books too. But to do so, we need to take advantage of another trick of the brain. In addition to reading more than one word at a time, we have to learn to read out of order.

Consider the following two lines from an obscure Victorian novel:

It is a truth universally acknowledged, that a single man
in possession of a good fortune must be in want of a wife.

If we were to try to read them at 2,000 wpm line by line then the points of fixation would be:

It is a truth universally a**X**cknowledged, that a single man

in possession of a good f**X**ortune must be in want of a wife.

To read at the same speed but ensure that all the words are sufficiently close to a fixation point, you would focus as follows: -

(It is a truth universally)(acknowledged, that a single man)
       X1   **X2**
(in possession of a good)(fortune must be in want of a wife).

Here your first point of focus is **X1** and your second is **X2**. As you can see you are having to read out of order: the first half of line one together with the first half of line two, then the second half of line one with the second half of line two. This way, no word is too far away from your point of focus. None of the words will be too blurry.

Using these points of focus, what your eye actually takes in and what you consciously experience is something akin to this:-

(It is a truth universally)
(in possession of a good)
(acknowledged, that a single man)
(fortune must be in want of a wife)

There is one obvious objection to reading like this and you have probably thought of it already. The words make no sense when seen out of order. However, the brain is more flexible than might be imagined.

Aoccdrnig to rscheearch at Cmabrigde Uinervtisy, it deosn't mttaer in waht oredr the ltteers in a wrod are, the olny iprmoatnt tihng is taht the frist and lsat ltteer be at the rghit pclae. The rset can be a toatl mses and you can sitll raed it wouthit a porbelm. Tihs is bcuseae the huamn mnid deos not raed ervey lteter by istlef, but the wrod as a wlohe

This paragraph was circulated as an internet meme a few years ago. As you can see it is not only possible, but quite easy, to read words where letters are out of order. The only requirement in this case is that the first and last letters of each word are in the correct place.

The same applies for reading sequences of words out of order. It is possible to do so and the brain will rearrange them so that the meaning becomes clear. Try with the following passage which we have rearranged in the same manner as we did with the lines from Pride & Prejudice. This passage is from the start of Gulliver's Travels.

My father had a small estate
third of five sons. He
in Nottinghamshire; I was the
sent me to Emanuel College

in Cambridge at fourteen years
years, and applied myself close
old, where I resided three
to my studies: but the

charge of maintaining me (although
allowance) being too great for
I had a very scanty
a narrow fortune, I was

bound apprentice to Mr. James
London, with whom I continued
Bates, an eminent surgeon in
four years; and my father

now and then sending me
laid them out in learning
small sums of money, I
navigation, and other parts of

the mathematics, useful to those
I always believed it would
who intend to travel, as
be some time or other

my fortune to do. When
went down to my father;
I left Mr. Bates, I
where, by the assistance of

him and my uncle John,
got forty pounds, and a
and some other relations I
promise of thirty pounds a

year to maintain me at
two years and seven months,
Leyden: there I studied physic
knowing it would be useful

in long voyages.
Leyden, I was recommended, by
Soon after my return from
my good master Mr. Bates,

to be surgeon to the
commander; with whom I continued
Swallow, Captain Abraham Pannell
three years and a half,

making a voyage or two
other parts. When I came
into the Levant, and some
back, I resolved to settle

in London, to which Mr.
me; and by him I was
Bates, my master, encouraged
recommended to several patients.

I took part of a small
and being advised to alter
house in the Old Jury,
my condition, I married Mrs.

Mary Burton, second daughter to
Newgate Street, with whom I
Mr. Edmond Burton, hosier, in
received four hundred pounds for

a portion.
dying in two years after, and
But, my good master Bates
I having few friends, my business

began to fail; for my conscience
imitate the bad practice of
would not suffer me to
too many among my brethren.

Having therefore consulted with my
acquaintance, I determined to go
wife, and some of my
again to sea. I was

surgeon successively in two ships,
six years, to the East
and made several voyages, for
and West Indies, by which

I got some addition to
leisure I spent in reading
my fortune. My hours of
the best authors, ancient and

modern, being always provided
books; and when I was
with a good number of
ashore, in observing the

manners and dispositions of
learning their language, wherein
the people, as well as
I had a great facility

by the strength of my
The last of these voyages
memory.
not proving very fortunate, I

grew weary of the sea,
home with my wife and family.
and intended to stay at

No doubt it felt a little odd to read this way, but were you able to understand what was going on? If you were, then you will at least in principle be able to read at speeds higher than 1,000wpm.

Practice

It will require practice to attain these higher speeds. We suggest that you use the practice regime we outlined in section nine for reaching 1,000 wpm. Make the one following adjustment: for each stage, rather than read one line at a time from your book, read two lines at a time. Then move down two lines, read those two, and so on.

You may want to take the pressure off yourself as you get accustomed to reading more than one line at a time as well as reading out of order. If it helps, switch off the metronome. However, once you are confident that you can read in this manner, re-introduce the metronome as it will help you achieve the higher speeds you want.

Onword

Having now shown you how to read at 2,000 wpm, we will go on to outline how you can read even faster, achieving speeds of 3,000 or 4,000 wpm.

ELEVEN

READING FASTER THAN 2,000 WPM

Exactly the same principles apply for faster speeds. To read at 3,000 wpm you will need to read three lines at a time. You will focus on one line, but take in information from the lines above and below as follows. As before, X marks the point of focus: -

(Mr Phileas Fogg lived, in 1872, at)(No. 7, Saville Row, Burlington)
(Gardens, the hXouse in which She)(ridan died in X1814. He was one of)
(the most noticeable members of the)(Reform Club, though he seemed)

(always to avoid attracting attention)(an enigmatical personage, about)
(whom little wasXknown, except that)(he was a poliXshed man of the)
(world. People said that he resembled)(Byron, - at least that his head)

(was Byronic; but he was a bearded)(tranquil Byron, who might live on)
(a thousand yearsXwithout growing o)(ld. Certainly anX Englishman, it)
(was more doubtful whether Phileas)(Fogg was a Londoner. He was never)

As you can see you initially focus on the middle of the first section of line two, taking in information from the first half of line one and line three as well, then you move on to focus on the second half of line two, taking in information from the second half of lines one and three.

What you subjectively experience may be something like this: -

(Mr Phileas Fogg lived, in 1872, at)
(Gardens, the hXouse in which)
(the most noticeable members of the)
(No. 7, Saville Row, Burlington)
(Sheridan died in X1814. He was one of)
(Reform Club, though he seemed)

Clearly it is getting harder to comprehend what is going on as the text is more jumbled that it was before but again with practice your brain can manage it.

Practice

To practice, adopt the same regime as you did for reaching 1,000 wpm, this time reading three lines at a time. By now you should understand the process for going ever faster. To read at 4,000 wpm you would have to take in four lines at a time, to read at 5,000 wpm, five lines at a time, and so on.

Just as there are only so many words that you can read to the left and right of the point of fixation without them becoming too blurry, so there are only so many lines you can read above and below. This places an upper limit on the number of words you can read in this manner. This limit is in the region of 5,000 wpm.

To read any faster, we are going to have to read in a slightly different way which might not be reading as you normally understand it. It will mean changing your approach still further.

Onword

In part four we look at different approaches to reading that will help you get through more material in less time. You can use combine these approaches with the speed reading techniques we have already outlined but it is not necessary to do so. For some people, therefore, these upcoming techniques will provide you with an alternative way of reading more quickly.

PART 4

INTELLIGENT READING

TWELVE

SCANNING AND SKIMMING

In the remaining chapters we are going to look at other techniques to help you read more quickly. The methods we have outlined so far can be very effective. However, they do require a certain amount of dedicated practice. The techniques we outline in this section are less intense but will still enable you to read large amounts of material in less time than you do now. If you have mastered the previous sections and can now read at vey high speeds, you can combine those skills with what we outline here to read even more quickly.

Scanning and Skimming

In the introduction we said that people who had been taught to skim read were able to do so at speeds of up to 20,000 wpm. In this section we are going to look at scanning and skimming and develop your skills in both. They should both become important elements in your arsenal of reading tools.

Scanning

Scanning is reading by searching specifically for a word, group of words or concept. This is not skill you will necessarily use when reading a novel, but you might need it when you are looking through material for a particular item, for instance a word, name or number. This is important because there will be many instances where you will have a certain amount of material to read, but you do not need to read all of it because you are simply looking for a particular piece of information.

Given our brain's capacity to take in information when it is primed to do so, you will actually take in more information from a piece of reading when you are searching for a specific item than when you are scanning through it aimlessly.

In the following exercises you will find sequences of numbers. The left most number is repeated somewhere else in the same row. Cover up all the rows and then reveal one row at a time. Your aim is to spot where in the row the left hand number is repeated.

We have included strings of two numbers which then increase to three, then four. Go as quickly as you can and record the time you take. If you want to develop your scanning skills you can use this exercise again, using different numbers that you have selected yourself.

Each exercise has nineteen sequences of numbers, so if you do produce your own exercise, we suggest that you also use sets of nineteen sequences so that you can reliably measure any increases in your scanning rate.

Scanning exercise - two numbers

38 32 79 50 28 84 19 71 69 38 93 75 10 72 45 87 00 66 06 31 55 88 17

48 81 10 55 59 64 46 22 94 54 93 03 81 96 48 28 81 09 56 65 93 34 46

12 84 75 64 82 33 78 67 83 16 52 71 12 19 09 14 56 48 56 69 23 46 03

48 61 04 54 32 66 48 21 33 93 60 72 60 24 91 41 27 30 00 56 48 27 14

41 02 70 41 38 52 10 46 65 21 38 41 46 95 19 31 51 16 09 49 83 36 73

36 24 92 30 78 16 40 62 86 20 89 98 62 80 34 82 53 42 36 70 67 98 21

48 08 65 13 28 72 45 87 78 66 06 31 55 88 17 48 81 20 92 09 62 82 92

54 09 54 15 36 43 67 89 25 90 36 00 11 33 05 30 24 88 24 66 21 38 41

46 95 19 41 51 16 09 43 30 57 27 03 65 75 95 91 95 30 92 16 11 73 46

32 61 17 93 10 51 18 54 80 32 46 23 79 96 27 49 56 73 51 88 57 52 72

48 91 22 79 48 83 01 19 49 12 98 33 67 33 62 44 06 56 64 08 60 21 39

49 46 39 52 24 73 71 90 70 21 79 49 60 94 37 02 77 05 39 21 71 76 29

31 76 75 23 84 67 48 18 46 76 69 40 51 32 31 05 68 12 71 45 26 35 60

82 77 85 77 13 47 57 78 60 91 73 63 71 78 72 82 68 44 09 01 40 65 66

43 08 60 21 39 49 46 39 52 24 73 71 90 70 21 79 86 09 43 70 27 70 53

92 17 17 62 93 10 49 95 10 59 73 17 32 81 60 96 31 85 92 02 44 59 45

53 46 90 83 02 64 25 22 30 53 43 34 46 85 03 52 61 93 11 88 17 10 10

00 31 37 83 87 52 88 65 87 53 32 08 38 14 20 61 71 77 66 91 47 00 35

98 25 34 90 42 87 55 46 87 31 15 95 62 86 38 82 30 66 47 93 98 60 95

Scanning exercise - 3 numbers

258 923 542 019 956 112 129 021 960 258 034 418 159 813 629 774 771

309 960 518 309 211 349 999 998 372 978 520 920 962 829 254 091 715

364 367 892 590 360 011 330 530 548 827 675 238 467 481 364 766 940

513 214 159 265 358 979 323 846 264 358 097 494 513 230 781 640 628

620 899 862 620 482 534 217 679 821 480 865 132 823 066 470 938 446

095 505 822 317 253 594 081 283 305 727 036 575 959 195 095 218 611

738 193 738 179 310 511 854 807 446 237 996 274 956 735 188 575 272

489 122 793 818 301 194 912 481 117 489 287 122 680 661 300 199 278

766 111 959 766 164 201 989 897 932 384 626 433 832 795 028 841 971

693 993 751 014 159 265 355 820 974 944 522 495 343 014 654 693 531

050 792 279 689 258 923 542 019 561 112 050 608 640 344 181 581 362

977 477 130 996 051 870 721 149 999 983 729 780 977 510 597 317 328

160 963 185 950 244 160 534 690 302 642 522 308 253 344 685 035 261

931 188 171 010 003 178 387 288 658 931 320 838 142 061 717 764 914

730 359 825 349 028 755 687 311 595 628 638 823 730 875 937 595 778

185 778 053 171 185 066 130 019 278 766 111 959 092 164 201 989 383

279 502 884 197 169 399 375 107 245 279 066 063 158 817 488 115 559

644 622 948 954 930 381 964 428 810 975 665 933 446 128 644 648 233

786 783 165 271 201 909 145 648 566 923 460 348 610 454 326 648 786

Scanning exercise - 4 numbers

7381 2138 4146 9519 4151 1609 4330 5727 0365 7595 9195 7381 1611 7381 9326

2724 3105 1185 4807 4462 3799 6274 9567 3518 8575 2724 8912 2793 8183 0119

0656 9833 6733 6244 0656 6430 8602 1394 9463 5224 7371 9070 2179 8609 4370

4674 5392 1717 6293 1767 5238 4674 8184 6766 9405 1320 0056 8127 1452 6356

7134 7857 7134 7577 8960 9173 6371 7872 1468 4409 0140 6566 4308 6021 3949

1732 5224 7371 9070 2179 8609 4370 2770 5392 1717 6293 1049 9510 5973 1732

0352 9631 8595 0244 5945 5346 9083 0264 2522 3082 5334 4685 0352 6193 1188

3137 1000 3137 8387 5288 6587 5332 0838 1420 6171 7766 9147 3035 9825 3490

6286 5546 8731 1595 6286 3882 3066 4793 8416 0955 0582 2317 2539 4081 2848

5665 4502 8410 2701 9385 2105 5596 4462 2948 9549 3038 1964 4288 1097 5665

4543 4612 8476 4823 3786 7831 6527 1201 9091 4564 8566 9234 6034 8610 4543

7260 2133 9360 7260 2491 4127 3235 3787 5937 5195 7781 8577 8053 2152 6356

3637 7857 7134 2757 7896 0917 3637 1787 2146 8440 9012 2495 3430 1465 4958

6086 5079 2279 6892 5892 3542 0199 5611 2129 0219 6086 4034 4181 5981 3629

9999 7130 9960 5187 0721 1349 9999 9837 2978 5209 2096 8292 5409 1715 3643

1415 2590 3600 1133 0530 5458 8276 7523 8467 4818 4676 6940 5132 1415 9265

3846 7932 3846 2643 5820 9749 4459 2307 8164 0628 6208 9986 2803 4825 3421

8446 9821 4808 6513 2823 0664 7093 8446 0955 0582 2317 2535 9408 1283 3057

7996 6575 9591 5953 0921 8611 7381 9326 1173 1051 1854 8074 4623 7996 2749

Advanced scanning exercises

The previous exercise is designed to train your eye and brain to look for specific information. However in most realistic reading situations, you will be looking for information other than numbers.

In this exercise you will practise scanning in a more realistic way. Over the page are extracts from Alice's Adventures in Wonderland and Around the World in Eighty Days. Below are ten words that appear in each and the number of times that they occur.

Scan through the extract looking for the first word on the list. When you have found it the required number of times, pick the next word and look for that one. Carry on until you have found all ten words. Work out how long it takes to find each word by dividing the total time taken by the total number of words. As before, you can use this exercise as a template to develop your own.

Extract 1:   Alice's Adventures in Wonderland

Alice	28	knife	1
minute(s)	2	table	5
curiosity	1	ignorant	1
mile(s)	2	candle	2
croquet	1	mouse	1

44 words in total.

Extract 2:   Around the World in Eighty Days

circular	1	surname	1
toilet	2	handsome	1
Passepartout	18	mansion	2
gentleman	3	owner	1
scientific	1	taciturn	1

31 words in total.

Alice's Adventures in Wonderland by Lewis Carroll

Christmas, 1867

DOWN THE RABBIT-HOLE

ALICE was beginning to get very tired of sitting by her sister on the bank and of having nothing to do: once or twice she had peeped into the book her sister was reading, but it had no pictures or conversations in it, 'and what is the use of a book,' thought Alice, 'without pictures or conversations?'

So she was considering, in her own mind (as well as she could, for the hot day made her feel very sleepy and stupid), whether the pleasure of making a daisy-chain would be worth the trouble of getting up and picking the daisies, when suddenly a White Rabbit with pink eyes ran close by her.

There was nothing so very remarkable in that; nor did Alice think it so very much out of the way to hear the Rabbit say to itself 'Oh dear! Oh dear! I shall be too late!' (when she thought it over afterwards it occurred to her that she ought to have wondered at this, but at the time it all seemed quite natural); but, when the Rabbit actually took a watch out of its waistcoat-pocket, and looked at it, and then hurried on, Alice started to her feet, for it flashed across her mind that she had never before seen a rabbit with either a waistcoat-pocket, or a watch to take out of it, and burning with curiosity, she ran across the field after it, and was just in time to see it pop down a large rabbit-hole under the hedge.

In another moment down went Alice after it, never once considering how in the world she was to get out again. The rabbit-hole went straight on like a tunnel for some way, and then dipped suddenly down, so suddenly that Alice had not a moment to think about stopping herself before she found herself falling down what seemed to be a very deep well.

Either the well was very deep, or she fell very slowly, for she had plenty of time as she went down to look about her, and to wonder what was going to happen next. First, she tried to look down and make out what she was coming to, but it was too dark to see anything: then she looked at the sides of the well, and noticed that they were filled with cupboards and bookshelves: here and there she saw maps and pictures hung upon pegs. She took down a jar from one of the shelves as she passed: it was labelled `ORANGE MARMALADE' but to her great disappointment it was empty: she did not like to drop the jar, for fear of killing somebody underneath, so managed to put it into one of the cupboards as she fell past it.

`Well!' thought Alice to herself. `After such a fall as this, I shall think nothing of tumbling down-stairs! How brave they'll all think me at home! Why, I wouldn't say anything about it, even if I fell off the top of the house!' (Which was very likely true.)

Down, down, down. Would the fall never come to an end? `I wonder how many miles I've fallen by this time?' she said aloud. `I must be getting somewhere near the centre of the earth. Let me see: that would be four thousand miles down, I think--' (for, you see, Alice had learnt several things of this sort in her lessons in the school-room, and though this was not a very good opportunity for showing off her knowledge, as there was no one to listen to her, still it was good practice to say it over) `--yes, that's about the right distance -- but then I wonder what Latitude or Longitude I've got to?' (Alice had not the slightest idea what Latitude was, or Longitude either, but she thought they were nice grand words to say.)

Presently she began again. `I wonder if I shall fall right through the earth! How funny it'll seem to come out among the people that walk with their heads downwards! The Antipathies, I think--' (she was rather glad there was no one listening, this time, as it didn't sound at all the right word) `-- but I shall have to ask them what the name of the country is, you know. Please, Ma'am, is this New Zealand? Or Australia?' (and she tried to curtsey as she spoke -- fancy, curtseying as you're falling through the air! Do you think you could manage it?) `And what an ignorant little girl she'll think me for asking! No, it'll never do to ask: perhaps I shall see it written up somewhere.'

Down, down, down. There was nothing else to do, so Alice soon began talking again. `Dinah'll miss me very much to-night, I should think!' (Dinah was the cat.) `I hope they'll remember her saucer of milk at tea-time. Dinah, my dear! I wish you were down here with me! There are no mice in the air, I'm afraid, but you might catch a bat, and that's very like a mouse, you know. But do cats eat bats, I wonder?' And here Alice began to get rather sleepy, and went on saying to herself, in a dreamy sort of way, `Do cats eat bats? Do cats eat bats?' and sometimes `Do bats eat cats?' for, you see, as she couldn't answer either question, it didn't much matter which way she put it. She felt that she was dozing off, and had just begun to dream that she was walking hand in hand with Dinah, and was saying to her, very earnestly, `Now, Dinah, tell me the truth: did you ever eat a bat?' when suddenly, thump! thump! down she came upon a heap of sticks and dry leaves, and the fall was over.

Alice was not a bit hurt, and she jumped up on to her feet in a moment: she looked up, but it was all dark overhead: before her was another long passage, and the White Rabbit was still in sight, hurrying down it. There was not a moment to be lost: away went Alice like the wind, and was just in time to hear it say, as it turned a corner, `Oh my ears and whiskers, how late it's getting!' She was close behind it when she turned the corner, but the Rabbit was no longer to be seen: she found herself in a long, low hall, which was lit up by a row of lamps hanging from the roof.

There were doors all round the hall, but they were all locked: and when Alice had been all the way down one side and up the other, trying every door, she walked sadly down the middle, wondering how she was ever to get out again.

Suddenly she came upon a little three-legged table, all made of solid glass: there was nothing on it but a tiny golden key, and Alice's first idea was that this might belong to one of the doors of the hall; but, alas! either the locks were too large, or the key was too small, but at any rate it would not open any of them. However, on the second time round, she came upon a low curtain she had not noticed before, and behind it was a little door about fifteen inches high: she tried the little golden key in the lock, and to her great delight it fitted!

Alice opened the door and found that it led into a small passage, not much larger than a rat-hole: she knelt down and looked along the passage into the loveliest garden you ever saw. How she longed to get out of that dark hall, and wander about among those beds of bright flowers and those cool fountains, but she could not even get her head through the doorway; `and even if my head would go through,' thought poor Alice, `it would be of very little use without my shoulders. Oh, how I wish I could shut up like a telescope! I think I could, if I only knew how to begin.' For, you see, so many out-of-the-way things had happened lately, that Alice had begun to think that very few things indeed were really impossible.

There seemed to be no use in waiting by the little door, so she went back to the table, half hoping she might find another key on it, or at any rate a book of rules for shutting people up like telescopes: this time she found a little bottle on it (`which certainly was not here before,' said Alice), and tied around the neck of the bottle was a paper label, with the words `DRINK ME' beautifully printed on it in large letters.

It was all very well to say `Drink me', but the wise little Alice was not going to do that in a hurry. `No, I'll look first,' she said, `and see whether it's marked `poison' or not'; for she had read several nice little stories about children who had got burnt, and eaten up by wild beasts, and other unpleasant things, all because they would not remember the simple rules their friends had taught them: such as, that a red-hot poker will burn you if you hold it too long; and that, if you cut your finger very deeply with a knife, it usually bleeds; and she had never forgotten that, if you drink much from a bottle marked `poison', it is almost certain to disagree with you, sooner or later.

However, this bottle was not marked `poison', so Alice ventured to taste it, and, finding it very nice (it had, in fact, a sort of mixed flavour of cherrytart, custard, pineapple, roast turkey, toffee, and hot buttered toast), she very soon finished it off.

*   *   *   *

  *   *   *

*   *   *   *

`What a curious feeling!' said Alice. `I must be shutting up like a telescope!'

And so it was indeed: she was now only ten inches high, and her face brightened up at the thought that she was now the right size for going through the little door into that lovely garden. First, however, she waited for a few minutes to see if she was going to shrink any further: she felt a little nervous about this; `for it might end, you know,' said Alice to herself, `in my going out altogether, like a candle. I wonder what I should be like then?' And she tried to fancy what the flame of a candle looks like after the candle is blown out, for she could not remember ever having seen such a thing.

After a while, finding that nothing more happened, she decided on going into the garden at once; but, alas for poor Alice! when she got to the door, she found she had forgotten the little golden key, and when she went back to the table for it, she found she could not possibly reach it: she could see it quite plainly through the glass, and she tried her best to climb up one of the legs of the table, but it was too slippery; and when she had tired herself out with trying, the poor little thing sat down and cried.

`Come, there's no use in crying like that!' said Alice to herself rather sharply. `I advise you to leave off this minute!' She generally gave herself very good advice (though she very seldom followed it), and sometimes she scolded herself so severely as to bring tears into her eyes; and once she remembered trying to box her own ears for having cheated herself in a game of croquet she was playing against herself, for this curious child was very fond of pretending to be two people. `But it's no use now,' thought poor Alice, `to pretend to be two people! Why, there's hardly enough of me left to make one respectable person!'

Soon her eye fell on a little glass box that was lying under the table: she opened it, and found in it a very small cake, on which the words `EAT ME' were beautifully marked in currants. `Well, I'll eat it,' said Alice, `and if it makes me grow larger, I can reach the key; and if it makes me grow smaller, I can creep under the door: so either way I'll get into the garden, and I don't care which happens!'

She ate a little bit, and said anxiously to herself `Which way? Which way?', holding her hand on the top of her head to feel which way it was growing; and she was quite surprised to find that she remained the same size. To be sure, this is what generally happens when one eats cake; but Alice had got so much into the way of expecting nothing but out-of-the-way things to happen, that it seemed quite dull and stupid for life to go on in the common way.

So she set to work, and very soon finished off the cake.

(2176 words)

Around the World in Eighty Days by Jules Verne

In Which Phileas Fogg And Passepartout Accept Each Other, The One As Master, The Other As Man.

Mr Phileas Fogg lived, in 1872, at No. 7, Saville Row, Burlington Gardens, the house in which Sheridan died in 1814. He was one of the most noticeable members of the Reform Club, though he seemed always to avoid attracting attention; an enigmatical personage, about whom little was known, except that he was a polished man of the world. People said that he resembled Byron, - at least that his head was Byronic; but he was a bearded, tranquil Byron, who might live on a thousand years without growing old.

Certainly an Englishman, it was more doubtful whether Phileas Fogg was a Londoner. He was never seen on `Change, nor at the Bank, nor in the counting-rooms of the `City'; no ships ever came into London docks of which he was the owner; he had no public employment; he had never been entered at any of the Inns of Court, either at the Temple, or Lincoln's Inn, or Gray's Inn; nor had his voice ever resounded in the Court of Chancery, or in the Exchequer, or the Queen's Bench, or the Ecclesiastical Courts. He certainly was not a manufacturer; nor was he a merchant or a gentleman farmer. His name was strange to the scientific and learned societies, and he never was known to take part in the sage deliberations of the Royal Institution or the London Institution, the Artisan's Association or the Institution of Arts and Sciences. He belonged, in fact, to none of the numerous societies which swarm in the English capital, from the Harmonic to that of the Entomologists, founded mainly for the purpose of abolishing pernicious insects. Phileas Fogg was a member of the Reform, and that was all.

The way in which he got admission to this exclusive club was simple enough.

He was recommended by the Barings, with whom he had an open credit. His cheques were regularly paid at sight from his account current, which was always flush.

Was Phileas Fogg rich? Undoubtedly. But those who knew him best could not imagine how he had made his fortune, and Mr Fogg was the last person to whom to apply for the information. He was not lavish, nor, on the contrary, avaricious; for whenever he knew that money was needed for a noble, useful, or benevolent purpose, he supplied it quietly and sometimes anonymously. He was, in short, the least communicative of men. He talked very little and seemed all the more mysterious for his taciturn manner. His daily habits were quite open to observation; but whatever he did was so exactly the same thing that he had always done before, that the wits of the curious were fairly puzzled.

Had he travelled? It was likely, for no one seemed to know the world more familiarly; there was no spot so secluded that he did not appear to have an intimate acquaintance with it. He often corrected, with a few clear words, the thousand conjectures advanced by members of the club as to lost and unheard- of travellers, pointing out the true probabilities, and seeming as if gifted with a sort of second sight, so often did events justify his predictions. He must have travelled everywhere, at least in the spirit.
It was at least certain that Phileas Fogg had not absented himself from London for many years. Those who were honoured by a better acquaintance with him than the rest, declared that nobody could pretend to have ever seen him anywhere else. His sole pastimes were reading the papers and playing whist. He often won at this game, which, as a silent one, harmonized with his nature; but his winnings never went into his purse, being reserved as a fund for his charities. Mr Fogg played, not to win, but for the sake of playing. The game was in his eyes a contest, struggle with a difficulty, yet a motionless, unwearying struggle, congenial to his tastes.

Phileas Fogg was not known to have either wife or children, which may happen to the most honest people; either relatives or near friends, which is certainly more unusual. He lived alone in his house in Saville Row, whither none penetrated. A single domestic sufficed to serve him. He breakfasted and dined at the club, at hours mathematically fixed, in the same room, at the same table, never taking his meals with other members, much less bringing a guest with him; and went home at exactly midnight, only to retire at once to bed. He never used the cosy chambers which the Reform provides for its favoured members. He passed ten hours out of the twenty-four in Saville Row, either in sleeping or making his toilet. When he chose to take a walk it was with a regular step in the entrance hall with its mosaic flooring, or in the circular gallery with its dome supported by twenty red porphyry Ionic columns, and illumined by blue painted windows. When he breakfasted or dined all the resources of the club - its kitchens and pantries, its buttery and dairy - aided to crowd his table with their most succulent stores; he was served by the gravest waiters, in dress coats, and shoes with swan-skin soles, who proffered the viands in special porcelain, and on the finest linen; club decanters, of a lost mould, contained his sherry, his port, and his cinnamon-spiced claret; while his beverages were refreshingly cooled with ice, brought at great cost from the American lakes. If to live in this style is to be eccentric, it must be confessed that there is something good in eccentricity.

The mansion in Saville Row, though not sumptuous, was exceedingly comfortable. The habits of its occupant were such as to demand but little from the sole domestic, but Phileas Fogg required him to be almost superhumanly prompt and regular. On this very 2nd of October he had dismissed James Forster, because that luckless youth had brought him shaving-water at eighty-four degrees Fahrenheit instead of eighty-six; and he was awaiting his successor, who was due at the house between eleven and half-past.

Phileas Fogg was seated squarely in his armchair, his feet close together like those of a grenadier on parade, his hands resting on his knees, his body straight, his head erect; he was steadily watching a complicated clock which indicated the hours, the minutes, the seconds, the days, the months, and the years. At exactly half-past eleven Mr Fogg would, according to his daily habit, quit Saville Row, and repair to the Reform.

A rap at this moment sounded on the door of the cosy apartment where Phileas Fogg was seated, and James Forster, the dismissed servant, appeared.

`The new servant,' said he. A young man of thirty advanced and bowed.

`You are a Frenchman, I believe,' asked Phileas Fogg, `and your name is John?'

`Jean, if monsieur pleases,' replied the newcomer, `Jean Passepartout, a surname which has clung to me because I have a natural aptness for going out of one business into another. I believe I'm honest, monsieur, but, to be outspoken, I've had several trades. I've been an itinerant singer, a circus -

rider, when I used to vault like Leotard, and dance on a rope like Blondin. Then I got to be a professor of gymnastics, so as to make better use of my talents; and then I was a sergeant fireman at Paris, and assisted at many a big fire. But I quitted France five years ago and, wishing to taste the sweets of domestic life, took service as a valet here in England. Finding myself out of place, and hearing that Monsieur Phileas Fogg was the most exact and settled gentleman in the United Kingdom, I have come to monsieur in the hope of living with him a tranquil life, and forgetting even the name of Passepartout.'

`Passepartout suits me,' responded Mr Fogg. `You are well recommended to me; I hear a good report of you. You know my conditions?'

`Yes, monsieur.'

`Good. What time is it?'

`Twenty - two minutes after eleven,' returned Passepartout, drawing an enormous silver watch from the depths of his pocket.

`You are too slow,' said Mr Fogg.

`Pardon me, monsieur, it is impossible--'

`You are four minutes too slow. No matter; it's enough to mention the error. Now from this moment, twenty- nine minutes after eleven, a.m., this Wednesday, October 2nd, you are in my service.'

Phileas Fogg got up, took his hat in his left hand, put it on his head with an automatic motion, and went off without a word.

Passepartout heard the street door shut once; it was his new master going out. He heard it shut again; it was his predecessor, James Forster, departing in his turn. Passepartout remained alone in the house in Saville Row.

In Which Passepartout Is Convinced That He Has At Last Found His Ideal.

`Faith,' muttered Passepartout, somewhat flurried, `I've seen people at Madame Tussaud's as lively as my new master!'

Madame Tussaud's `people,' let it be said, are of wax, and are much visited in London; speech is all that is wanting to make them human.

During his brief interview with Mr Fogg, Passepartout had been carefully observing him. He appeared to be a man about forty years of age, with fine, handsome features, and a tall, well - shaped figure; his hair and whiskers were light, his forehead compact and unwrinkled, his face rather pale, his teeth magnificent. His countenance possessed in the highest degree what physiognomists call `repose in action,' a quality of those who act rather than talk. Calm and phlegmatic, with a clear eye, Mr Fogg seemed a perfect type of that English composure which Angelica Kauffmann has so skilfully represented on canvas. Seen in the various phases of his daily life, he gave the idea of being perfectly well-balanced, as exactly regulated as a Leroy chronometer. Phileas Fogg was, indeed, exactitude personified, and this was betrayed even in the expression of his very hands and feet; for in men, as well as in animals, the limbs themselves are expressive of the passions.

He was so exact that he was never in a hurry, was always ready, and was economical alike of his steps and his motions. He never took one step too many, and always went to his destination by the shortest cut; he made no superfluous gestures, and was never seen to be moved or agitated. He was the most deliberate person in the world, yet always reached his destination at the exact moment.

He lived alone, and so to speak, outside of every social relation; and as he knew that in this world account must be taken of friction, and that friction retards, he never rubbed against anybody.

As for Passepartout, he was a true Parisian of Paris. Since he had abandoned his own country for England, taking service as a valet, he had in vain searched for a master after his own heart. Passepartout was by no means one of those pert dunces depicted by Molière, with a bold gaze and a nose held high in the air; he was an honest fellow, with a pleasant face, lips a trifle protruding, soft - mannered and serviceable, with a good round head, such as one likes to see on the shoulders of a friend. His eyes were blue, his complexion rubicund, his figure almost portly and well - built, his body muscular, and his physical powers fully developed by the exercises of his younger days. His brown hair was somewhat tumbled; for while the ancient sculptors are said to have known eighteen methods of arranging Minerva's tresses, Passepartout was familiar with but one of dressing his own: three strokes of a large - tooth comb completed his toilet.

It would be rash to predict how Passepartout's lively nature would agree with Mr Fogg. It was impossible to tell whether the new servant would turn out as absolutely methodical as his master required; experience alone could solve the question. Passepartout had been a sort of vagrant in his early years, and now yearned for repose; but so far he had failed to find it, though he had already served in ten English houses. But he could not take root in any of these; with chagrin he found his masters invariably whimsical and irregular, constantly running about the country, or on the look-out for adventure. His last master, young Lord Longferry, Member of Parliament, after passing his nights in the Haymarket taverns, was too often brought home in the morning on policemen's shoulders. Passepartout, desirous of respecting the gentleman whom he served, ventured a mild remonstrance on such conduct; which being ill-received, he took his leave. Hearing that Mr Phileas Fogg was looking for a servant, and that his life was one of unbroken regularity, that he neither travelled nor stayed from home overnight, he felt sure that this would be the place he was after. He presented himself, and was accepted, as has been seen.

At half-past eleven, then, Passepartout found himself alone in the house in Saville Row. He began its inspection without delay, scouring it from cellar to garret. So clean, well-arranged, solemn a mansion pleased him; it seemed to him like a snail's shell, lighted and warmed by gas, which sufficed for both these purposes. When Passepartout reached the second storey he recognized at once the room which he was to inhabit, and he was well satisfied with it. Electric bells and speaking tubes afforded communication.

(2267 words)

Skimming

The aim of skimming is to help you to preview material at high speeds. By previewing material, you will see all of the material you are planning to read in a very short space of time, and even if you do not take it all in, you will gain an idea of the structure and content of the material you will be reading.

As you skim, your brain will start making subconscious connections between what you are seeing and knowledge you already have. This will make it easier to absorb information when you read through more thoroughly later on. We suggest that you preview all material you read, with the exception of any reading purely for pleasure where you want to be surprised by what comes next.

In this exercise we suggest you use a non-fiction book with diagrams and pictures or alternatively a magazine or newspaper. If you are using a book start at the beginning of chapter one; if a magazine start at the first article; if a newspaper, start with the front page.

Turn on your metronome and set it to the rate that you usually use.

Using your visual guide, move it over each page at the rate of one page per second and allow your eyes to follow it. Start your guide off at the top left hand corner of the left hand page and move it diagonally to the bottom right hand corner of the same page. Then move on to the right hand page, start at the bottom left corner, and move diagonally up to the top right. Your pen will describe a V-shape as it moves over a pair of pages.

If you are using a fixation rate of four fixations per second, you will be making four fixations on each page. Do this for about two minutes.

When you have finished spend some time reviewing the exercise. You may not have taken in a huge amount of detailed information, yet you will have gained a great deal of generalised information.

Your eye will have picked out headlines, chapter headings and the occasional word from within a paragraph. You will get an overview of the structure of the text. You will see whether there are any pictures, diagrams or tables so you will know where to direct your attention later on when come to read in more detail.

You will also notice things like the type and size of font which will give you an idea of how easy the text will be to read. Depending on the piece you used you may have noticed whether there were footnotes on the pages and depending on whether you read footnotes or not, this will affect how much reading there is to do.

For some books you may notice that different sub-sections of text are in different colours, indicating different types of material.

All of this will be priming your brain so that when you read the material in more detail later on it will be easier, faster and you will take more in.

Skimming practice

Set aside some time each day to practise skimming. As with any of the reading skills we have outlined in this course, the more you practise the better you will become. One easy way of ensuring that you skim every day is to skim read the newspaper. This will also ensure that you have an overview of the previous day's news and let you know which articles you want to read.

Onword

Having outlined scanning and skimming we are going to show how to incorporate these skills into a larger whole that will enable you to read more material effectively in less time. Before that, though, we will outline some ways of ensuring that you mind is fully engaged when reading.

THIRTEEN

INVOLVING YOUR CRITICAL FACULTIES

One of the main ways that you can get more out of your reading is to ensure that you fully understand the text. Lack of understanding can lead to a decrease in motivation to read, and thus a reduction in speed. You may get bogged down and not want to pursue your reading any further.

There are various different levels at which any piece of writing can be understood (or misunderstood):

Letter recognition

The most basic level of understanding is the recognition of the characters that make up the words being used. We assume that you are already able to do this to a high level or you would not be reading this now. However, implicit in this is an assumption that you can actually see what you are reading. If your eyes are not up to the task, then you will find that your understanding is limited. If you think that your eyesight is defective in any way, we suggest that you consult an optician.

Word recognition

The next level of understanding is that of individual words: you may find that your understanding is limited by a poor knowledge of the English language. If so, we suggest that you take steps to broaden your vocabulary. One easy way of doing this is to have a dictionary to hand whenever you read and look up any words that you do not understand or where you are not completely sure of the meaning. Another way is simply to read more.

Meaning

Moving on to a higher level of meaning, we come to an understanding of what the words, phrases and sentences you are reading actually mean. This involves a range of academic subjects such as epistemology, philology, linguistics and philosophy of language.

Here we merely summarise some points to bear in mind: -

• The writer is trying to convey some sort of idea to the reader. Is this idea stated explicitly in the text? That is, is it literal? If not, how do we know what the writer is trying to say? Is it implied? If it is implied, why is that the case? Is there a reason for not stating it explicitly? Is the idea considered too obvious to state. The writer may assume a degree of common knowledge with the reader. However, the writer's experience of the world will inevitably be different from the reader's, so this assumption might be misplaced. If you don't understand something because your assumptions differ from the writer's, don't be afraid to challenge the writer's view of the world.

• Remember, also, that whether the meaning is express or implied has no bearing on whether or not it is true. Many people are inclined to believe what they read merely because it is in print.

• Another reason that an idea may not be expressed explicitly is that the author may be lacking confidence in the idea or may be embarrassed about stating it. Bear this in mind when reading and consider whether this has any impact on the writer's credibility. Alternatively, it may be the case that the author hasn't thought to question his own assumptions. We all live by assumptions that we don't challenge. Life would too complicated if we did. But sometimes doing so can be fruitful. For instance, by challenging everyone's assumptions about the inflexibility of time and space, Einstein came up with his theories of relativity.

A good approach to understanding at this level of meaning is to adopt a critical and questioning approach. As you read, question what the author is saying. Does what he says make sense? Has he adopted any underlying assumptions? Is he assuming certain knowledge on the reader's part? If so, what? Taking such an approach will increase your emotional and logical involvement with your reading and make it more memorable.

If you have read our courses on memory you will know that you can increase your chances of remembering something by involving your whole brain. Switching on your critical faculties will help you do this. If you would like to find out more about developing your critical thinking skills, take a look at our Analytical Thinking Quick Course.

Onword

In the next section we will move on to outline a series of steps you can take that will help you get through large amounts of information very quickly. Make sure that you use both the skimming and scanning skills we have outlined and that your critical facilities are engaged for any reading that you do.

FOURTEEN

NON-LINEAR READING

The aim of this section is to give you various strategies to help you manage your reading, so that you can better decide how to direct your attention; what to read and what to ignore; and how to be in the best position to put what you read to good use. You can use the strategies here with all different types of reading tasks, including non-fiction books, articles, study materials, letters and reports.

Most books and other types of reading material, with the exception fiction, do not need to be read from the first page to the last page, page by page. Instead you can jump in and out at the points that are most useful. You can even look at material that comes later in the text before earlier material. It depends entirely on what you consider important.

Our aim here is to focus our attention in a laser-like manner specifically on the information that we need and only that information. We will omit anything that is not relevant or not important.

We are going to do this by taking in information going from the general to the specific. Try this exercise. See if you can mentally identify all of the instruments in a classical orchestra. Spend a short amount of time doing this.

When you have finished think about your strategy for doing so. What you probably did was think about a specific section of the orchestra, say strings – and then thought about the instruments in that section running from the highest, violin, down to the lowest, double-bass.

In other words you sought out categories starting at the most general level – the different sections of the orchestra – and then moved to specifics – the actual instruments. The tendency to categorise ideas in this way is a natural function of the human brain and so it is something we should use.

This makes it much easier for our brain to take in information. We are going to make use of this capacity now by taking in general information and using that information as hooks to add more and more detail.

We suggest that you use the following stages: -

Preparation

Skim through the material you want to read very quickly in order to preview it. Then decide how much time you want to devote to it and how much material you want to cover. Be realistic about the amount of material you will cover in the time you have available. Factors to bear in mind are the difficultly of the material, your familiarity with it, your ability and your previous knowledge in the area.

Priming

Make a note of what you already know about the subject matter. This will give you mental hooks to which you can attach the new material. Then quickly brainstorm what you already know about the material.

Finally, decide what exactly you want to get from the new material. Establish your goals with as much clarity as you can, so that you will know when you have achieved them. Why are you are reading this material? What do you hope to get out of it? When doing this, make sure that your goals relate to the content of the material. Do not, for example, state that you are reading it because your tutor or your boss has told you to. This will not help you ascertain which material to focus on.

Keep in mind your goals when you are reading the material at subsequent stages.

General overview

You are now going to move on to the material itself. This will let you know exactly what it is you are looking at, what you can expect to get out of it and enable you to focus on important sources of information.

Remember your aim is to move from the general to the specific.

Let us suppose that you have decided to read some chapters from a textbook. Before you read them, look at the front and rear covers as well as the table of contents. This will provide you with general information and give you an idea as to where to direct your focus.

Also examine the preface, foreword and introduction: these will give you the writer's view of the material.

The introduction may contain an overview or short summary of the book as a whole and as such may give you all the information you need depending on how much detail you want.

Also, if there is new relevant information that is not sufficient to require a rewrite of the book, it may have been added here.

When you have completed this stage, make any notes that you think appropriate.

Skimming / Scanning stage

Having read the material that precedes the actual content of the book (the contents, introduction, etc.) you are now going to move onto the actual material you have decided to read.

Firstly, skim the chapters you have selected at the rate of one page a second as outlined in the earlier section on skim reading. As discussed there, you will discover a great deal of information contained in those chapters. Is there a précis of the chapter at the beginning? How is the chapter laid out? Are there subdivisions that you can focus on? Are there diagrams, pictures, photographs? Are there footnotes? Is there a summary of the chapter at the end?

As you do this have a soft pencil handy. Is there anything that jumps out at you as important? If so, make a pencil mark at the appropriate place.

When you have done this scan read the selected chapters. Think about your goals for the reading and select the most important words or concepts. Have these in mind when you scan. Be on the lookout for any specific words or concepts that relate to these goals. Again, when you spot them, mark the appropriate place with a pencil.

When you have completed this stage, add to your notes if appropriate.

Read the selected material

When you have completed this overview, read the selected material in more detail. However, make sure that you only read the relevant material. Not all of the paragraphs, sentences or even words will be of equal importance. Some will be important and relevant, some will not. It is your aim to focus on those that are and devote your time to those, and avoid those that are not.

Here are some pointers as to how you can determine where to focus.

Your notes
You should have marked much of the important material as you skimmed and scanned. These will give you some idea of where to focus.

Summaries
Depending on the book (or whatever material you are reading) each chapter may contain a précis at the start, outlining what is to come. This will provide you with a little more information. Additionally, it may guide you to other areas of the chapter that are important. The same applies if there is a summary at the end of a chapter.

Headings
The headings of sub-divisions within the chapter will clearly help you in determining where to direct your attention.

Primacy and recency effects
If you are familiar with our memory courses you will know about these. We tend to remember more from the beginning or end of an event than what came in the middle. The same cognitive bias often applies to writers. They will often put what they consider most important at the start or the end of their writing: this applies at the level of the book itself, but also at the level of the chapter, paragraph and even sentence. Use this knowledge as a guide as to where to direct your attention.

Paragraph structure

You can use knowledge of paragraph structure to make better decisions about where to direct your attention. Just as you do not need to read every single word with the same degree of attention, the same with paragraphs. Some are more important than others, and you can use your knowledge of the different types of paragraph to decide where to concentrate: -

An explanatory paragraph will typically start with the idea to be explained. The middle section will link the ideas in what is hopefully a logical manner. The final sentence will be some sort of conclusion. Explanatory paragraphs are relatively important and therefore you should devote a high degree of attention to them.

Descriptive paragraphs: these are subsidiary to explanatory paragraphs. They may reiterate the same idea with the aim of increasing comprehension. Alternatively, they may provide an example to demonstrate the idea, which, if you already understand the concept under discussion, you might want to skip over.

Concluding paragraphs: coming at the end of a sequence, these will summarise the main ideas or arguments under discussion, and maybe give you an idea of the writer's opinion. These can, therefore, be very important.

Making sure that you focus on the different types of paragraph as you read will maintain your involvement with the material and thereby increase your understanding.

Fast reading

Using these approaches will help you to focus down directly on the specific information you want. Now you are going to read it in detail.

Using your visual guide, read through the selected material at high speed. If you have mastered reading at 1,000 wpm or more, this is the time to apply those techniques. Your aim here is to become aware more deeply of the structure of the material and focus on the important points.

Be aware that if the text is conceptually difficult or contains complicated language then you may read more slowly than you did for the light reading novel you used as practice.

Once you have established your appropriate reading speed for this material, do not slow down for difficult material. If there is material that you do not understand, mark it lightly with a pencil and leave it for the next stage. Your aim at this stage is to build a general mental structure.

Context is very important for understanding. If you stop to attempt to understand whenever you reach difficult material, you will only be deriving context from the material that preceded it, not what comes afterwards. By reading through all of the selected material, you ensure that you get the full context.

As before, make any further notes that you need to.

Detailed reading

Now conduct a detailed examination of the material. By now you should be quite familiar with it. It is at this stage that you focus on the main information in the material and fill in any blanks in your knowledge. It is here that you should attempt to understand any conceptually difficult material. As we outlined in the preceding chapters, ensure that you have your critical faculties fully engaged.

As you go through the material, mark anything you want to note with a soft pencil. At this stage you should make any detailed notes that you need to. One way of making notes (covered in more detail in our Mind Maps Quick Course) is to note the primary and secondary ideas from any paragraph that you want to note in keyword form. This will ensure that you focus on the important ideas and eliminate extraneous ones.

Review

Now that you have read the material in detail, you are nearly finished. However, before you stop, conduct a review of the material. This will help you to fix it in memory and enable you to resolve any remaining difficulties. At the priming stage you conducted a knowledge brainstorm.

You should now know more than you did before so repeat this exercise, checking that your knowledge base has indeed expanded.

Look back at your goals. Ask yourself if you have achieved them. If you have then your reading has been successful. If not, then you should consider whether your approach needs adjusting or whether the material you read was not appropriate and attempt to find something else to read on the same subject instead. Also, you might reconsider your goals. They may have changed as a result of the reading itself. Do not feel that you have to be a slave to the goals you set yourself before you undertook the reading.

Onword

This chapter has been concerned with the kinds of material that you can read in a non-linear fashion, which is virtually any material that is not a novel or story of some kind. We look briefly at fiction in general in the following chapter.

FIFTEEN

GETTING MORE OUT OF NOVELS

For fictional material such as novels and short stories, you will usually want to read them in page order so that the story unfolds as intended. However, even with fiction there are times when you might flip ahead a few pages, for example if you are checking if the material is appropriate for a child to read.

Lack of interest may be another reason to skip ahead. For instance, a thriller writer might write in extreme detail about the workings of a nuclear bomb, which isn't directly relevant to the plot. If you are not interested in knowing how a bomb works, you might skip over these pages and resume reading afterwards.

Topics to focus on

To ensure that you get the most out of your experience when reading works of fiction, you can concentrate on various different topics to maintain interest and motivation. Among these are the following: -

Plot or storyline

How important is the actual plot or story line? In some novels, particularly, thrillers and mysteries, plot is most important and character development is secondary. Ask yourself does the plot hold together in a logical manner?

Philosophical system

What is the philosophical system underlying the work? Few novels set out an explicit philosophical stance. However, some raise philosophical questions: for instance, works by Dostoyevsky and Sartre deal with ethical matters. Other works deal with political philosophy, such as George Orwell's, 1984 and Animal Farm. Some deal with metaphysics, such as Martin Amis's Time's Arrow and any number of science fiction works.

It is possible to question every work of literature from a philosophical standpoint, because they all assume the existence of a world that is different in some way from the actual word. Ask yourself to what extent is a fictional world that does not really exist capable of having any meaning at all? What assumptions do you need to make to buy into the story?

Standpoint

Another factor to take into consideration is the standpoint from which the book is written. Is it written in the third person or the first person? Examples of the latter are The Adventures of Huckleberry Finn by Mark Twain and Gulliver's Travels by Jonathan Swift. You might ask to what extent the words written and the views presented are those of the fictional author (Finn / Gulliver) or of the real author (Twain / Swift).

Character development

Just as some books concentrate on plot development, other concentrate on the development of the various characters. See the works of Charles Dickens for examples. You can use the idiosyncrasies and the catchphrases of the different characters as hooks to remember them and their situations. Other books devote relatively little time to character development. These present more opportunities for you to use your own imagination and creativity.

Mood

Some books are written in a very realistic prose style, including mundane details of the protagonists' lives. See, for example, Remembrance of Things Past by Proust. Others, such as One Hundred Years of Solitude by Gabriel Garcia Marquez, convey an air of unreality which affects the mood of the whole book.

Setting

The setting of the book is its physical or temporal location. What is the physical setting of the book? Which country is it set in? Is it set mainly indoors or outdoors? How does the setting affect the mood? King Lear (William Shakespeare) and Wuthering Heights (Emily Brontë) are examples of works where the various locations create a mood and relate significantly to other facets of the work. For instance, the two houses in Wuthering Heights are symbolic of Heathcliff and Cathy's different characters.

You might also consider the temporal setting. When is the novel set? This will determine the cultural setting of the characters and what might realistically be expected of them. The status of women in Victorian novels is very different from what it is today, and is usually inextricably linked to the development of the plot. Pride and Prejudice is a supreme example of this.

Literary Devices

You can look out for various literary devices used by the author, such as simile (when one thing is likened to another) and metaphor (when one thing actually stands for another). You can also look out for the use of imagery, when the author uses visual (or other sense related) words to convey his or her meaning. Symbolic imagery can also be used. A symbolic image is one in which a symbol stands for something else in the work: for example, in Freudian psychology, certain objects such as trains and tall buildings are phallic symbols.

Onword

We have now covered all of the topics necessary to ensure that you can read at significantly higher speeds. In the following section we outline some ideas as to how you can maintain the gains you make.

SIXTEEN

ONGOING PRACTICE

If you practise the exercises outlined in this course you will undoubtedly notice a considerable improvement in your reading speed. Your overall aim is to train your brain to get used to taking in information much more quickly than it is used to and this will take a little time.

Some of our other courses will also come in useful. As we have stated elsewhere, you will maximise your chances of being in the right mental state by familiarising yourself with our Concentration & Focus Quick Course, while the Visualisation Quick Course will help you to make mental pictures of what you read.

Our courses on healthy living will ensure that your brain is in the best condition that it can be in, while our courses on memory will help you retain information more easily. Our Mind Maps Quick Course will help you to make better notes.

To ensure that you make the maximum gains you can, you must practise regularly: it is always better to do a little practice every day, rather than go for days without doing anything and then spend hours trying to make up the time.

To ensure that you practise regularly, plan each session in advance, preferably the day before, so you are not distracted by the events of the day. Also, by doing this, there is less likelihood that you will omit a session due to other commitments.

You might like to experiment with working out what is the best time of day to have your practice sessions. However, when you have identified the time of day that suits you best, try to stick with it. This way it will become a natural habit.

We suggest that your practice sessions last between twenty minutes and an hour. By spending what is only a relatively short period of time on reading practice, you increase the likelihood that will actually do it, ensure your concentration levels stay high throughout and get the most out of each session.

When you plan, decide which reading exercises you want to work on. If you have enough time to cover them all, do so, but if not just focus on a few, and cover the remaining ones the next time round. Try always to include the basic exercises – practising with a visual guide, using a metronome and expanding your focus - as these are the fundamentals of improved technique: strengthening your eye muscles, directing your eyes to the correct place, increasing the number of fixations per second and increasing the number of words you take in per fixation.

Also, include in your practice the reading exercises designed to help you read at 1,000 wpm, as this means that you will be practising with a real book in an actual reading situation.

Reassess your natural reading speed every two weeks and make a note of this. This way you will always have a record of your progress.

Whenever you are reading, push yourself a little bit harder and faster each and every day. Don't ever rest on your laurels. To achieve excellence in any field you must constantly strive to do better and this applies to reading as well.

Whenever you practise, keep a notebook handy, and write down anything that you think is important. If something works well, make a note of it. If something doesn't work for you, make a note of that too.

Reviewing your reading progress

Every three months or so, assess the progress you have made. Write down what you think you have gained from your training and what benefits they have brought to you in your life.

Write down anything else that occurs to you as well. Also note down what you think you will gain from continuing with your speed reading training and identify what would happen if you gave up. Use these notes as a source of motivation to continue with your practice.

SEVENTEEN

ENDWORD

We have now been through the essentials of reading at speed and the essentials of good reading practice. You should now be able to read at very high speeds. Remember, however, that any skill requires effort to maintain it, so ensure that you conduct sufficient practice to fulfil your reading goals and take your reading to the next level.

Records

You might like to keep an ongoing record of what you read, when you read and any other related thoughts. This will act as a memory aid and also provide a ready source of information that you may be able to use in other areas of your life.

Happy reading!

More Quick Courses Coming Soon!

Visualisation

Analytical Thinking

Creative Thinking

Setting and Achieving Goals

Powerful States of Mind

Essential Communication Skills

Modelling Success

Healthy Eating

Healthy Sleep

Printed in Great Britain
by Amazon

59093899R00071